© [2024] Ethan W. Sage

All rights reserved. No part of this book may be reproduced, in any form or by any means, including electronic, mechanical, photocopying, recording, or otherwise, without the prior written permission of the publisher, except for brief excerpts used in reviews.

Disclaimer: The information contained in this book is for educational purposes only. While every effort has been made to ensure the accuracy of the content, the author and publisher disclaim any responsibility for errors or omissions. Readers are encouraged to seek professional advice where needed.

Retrieval-Augmented Generation for NLP Practitioners

Practical Projects for Building Intelligent Systems and Cutting-Edge Applications

By

Ethan W. Sage

Contents

Chapter 1: Introduction to Retrieval-Augmented Generation (RAG) **8**

What is Retrieval-Augmented Generation? 9

The Role of RAG in Modern NLP 15

Real-World Applications of RAG 20

Practical Exercise: Build a Simple RAG Workflow 21

Chapter 2: Understanding the Foundations **38**

2.1 Large Language Models (LLMs): Capabilities and Limitations 38

2.2 Knowledge Bases: Structured, Unstructured, and Hybrid Approaches 50

2.3 Fundamentals of Information Retrieval 62

2.4 How RAG Combines Retrieval and Generation 76

Chapter 3. Getting Started with RAG .. 90

3.1 Tools and Libraries for RAG Development 90

3.2 Installing and Configuring Python, FAISS, LangChain, and ElasticSearch 101

3.3 Setting Up Pretrained LLMs (OpenAI, Hugging Face, etc.) 113

3.4 Creating Your First RAG Workflow 126

Chapter 4. Building the RAG Architecture 139

4.1 The Two-Stage Pipeline: Retriever and Generator Explained 139

4.2 Designing the Retriever: Indexing and Querying Data 152

4.3 Connecting the Generator: Generating Context-Aware Responses 164

4.4 Optimizing for Scalability and Performance 179

Chapter 5. Practical Hands-On Projects 196

5.1 FAQ Retrieval System......................196

5.2 Conversational AI with RAG.........207

5.3 RAG for Summarizing Large Datasets 222

Chapter 6. Advanced Techniques and Optimizations 236

6.1 Enhancing Retrieval Accuracy with Dense Embeddings 236

6.2 Fine-Tuning Generative Models for Domain-Specific Knowledge 250

6.3 Scaling RAG Systems for Enterprise Applications 263

6.4 Reducing Latency for Real-Time Applications 275

Chapter 7. Best Practices for RAG Development..293

7.1 Preventing Hallucinations in LLM Outputs..293

7.2 Handling Noisy and Ambiguous Data 309

7.3 Securing Sensitive Data in RAG Pipelines 325

7.4 Evaluating and Debugging RAG Systems..342

Chapter 8. Future Directions for RAG 359

8.1 Emerging Trends in Retrieval-Augmented Generation 359

8.2 Integrating Multimodal Data with RAG 362

8.3 Advances in Embedding Models and Search Algorithms 366

8.4 Ethical Considerations: Bias, Privacy, and Responsible AI.................369

Chapter 9. Appendix 373

9.1 Code Snippets and Examples 373

9.2 Resources and References 383

9.3 Glossary of Terms 384

Chapter 1: Introduction to Retrieval-Augmented Generation (RAG)

Retrieval-Augmented Generation (RAG) is a fascinating and transformative concept in modern Natural Language Processing (NLP). It represents a marriage of two powerful ideas: **retrieving relevant knowledge** and **using large language models (LLMs) to generate human-like responses.** Whether you're a complete beginner curious about the future of NLP or an experienced practitioner looking for ways to enhance your AI systems, this chapter will provide you with a solid foundation.

By the end of this chapter, you will:

1. Understand what RAG is and why it matters.

2. Appreciate its role in modern NLP.

3. Learn about its benefits and challenges.

4. Discover real-world applications of RAG.

5. Try out practical exercises to get hands-on experience.

What is Retrieval-Augmented Generation?

Retrieval-Augmented Generation (RAG) is an innovative approach in Natural Language Processing (NLP) that blends two core ideas: **retrieving relevant information from external sources** and **using language models to generate informed, context-rich responses.** At its heart, RAG solves one of the biggest limitations of large language models (LLMs): their inability to access up-to-date or domain-specific knowledge outside their training data.

This hybrid method has become a powerful tool for building intelligent systems, as it allows LLMs to provide accurate and contextually relevant answers by fetching real-time information from a connected knowledge base. Let's break it down step by step to understand how RAG works, its benefits, challenges, and practical applications.

Breaking Down Retrieval-Augmented Generation

Key Components of RAG

1. **Retriever**
    - The retriever is responsible for searching and fetching relevant data from an external knowledge base.

- Tools like FAISS (for dense vector retrieval) or ElasticSearch (for sparse keyword-based search) are commonly used.

2. **Generator**

    - The generator uses the retrieved information to produce a response. It's typically a large language model such as GPT or BERT, which transforms the raw data into coherent, human-like text.

How RAG Works

1. A user sends a query or prompt to the system.

2. The retriever searches for the most relevant documents or data points from a connected knowledge base.

3. The generator takes the retrieved documents as additional context and produces a response that incorporates both the query and the retrieved information.

Why is RAG Important?

Large language models are trained on static datasets and cannot dynamically update their knowledge. As a result, they may fail when asked about recent events or niche topics. RAG addresses this limitation by connecting LLMs to **dynamic, queryable knowledge bases**, allowing them to:

- Provide accurate, real-time information.

- Handle specialized queries that require domain-specific knowledge.

- Deliver responses grounded in factual data rather than relying solely on probabilistic generation.

Benefits of RAG

1. **Dynamic Knowledge Integration**
   RAG allows systems to include the latest information without retraining the LLM. For example, a chatbot built with RAG can answer questions about news articles published moments ago.

2. **Domain-Specific Expertise**
   By connecting to specialized knowledge bases, RAG enables language models to act as experts in fields like medicine, law, or finance.

3. **Enhanced Accuracy**
   Retrieval ensures that the model's responses are grounded in factual

information, reducing the risk of generating incorrect or hallucinated content.

Challenges in RAG

1. **Retrieval Quality**
   The retriever must return highly relevant and accurate documents. Irrelevant results can lead to poor responses.

2. **Latency**
   Combining retrieval with generation adds processing time, which can affect performance in real-time applications.

3. **Complexity**
   Building and maintaining RAG pipelines require expertise in both NLP and information retrieval.

The Role of RAG in Modern NLP

Natural Language Processing (NLP) has seen tremendous advancements with the advent of large language models (LLMs). However, as powerful as these models are, they face certain limitations when applied to real-world problems. Retrieval-Augmented Generation (RAG) bridges some of these gaps, making it a pivotal innovation in the modern NLP landscape.

RAG enables NLP systems to leverage external knowledge bases, making them more accurate, flexible, and useful for a wide range of applications. This chapter delves into the critical roles RAG plays in NLP today, including enhancing accuracy, providing domain-specific expertise, and enabling dynamic knowledge integration.

Key Roles of RAG in NLP

1. Enhancing Accuracy

One of the most significant challenges in LLMs is the phenomenon of hallucination — when a model confidently generates incorrect or fabricated information. RAG mitigates this by grounding responses in retrieved, fact-checked data. This ensures that the generated output is both relevant and reliable.

For example:

- A medical chatbot using RAG can retrieve verified medical literature to answer questions, reducing the risk of incorrect advice.
- A legal assistant can pull case laws or statutory references directly from a database to inform its responses.

2. Enabling Domain-Specific Expertise

RAG allows NLP systems to cater to niche domains without retraining massive models. By integrating specialized knowledge bases, the system can provide expert-level responses tailored to specific industries or fields.

For instance:

- In **finance**, a system equipped with RAG can retrieve and analyze the latest market reports.
- In **education**, it can pull resources like textbooks or research papers to answer subject-specific questions.

3. Supporting Dynamic Knowledge Integration

LLMs, once trained, cannot update their knowledge base without expensive retraining. RAG addresses this limitation by enabling systems to fetch real-time information. This makes it ideal for:

- **News summarization**, where the model pulls live updates from trusted sources.
- **Customer support**, where it retrieves product information from a dynamic database.

Real-World Use Cases of RAG

A. Conversational AI

RAG-powered chatbots can deliver more intelligent and accurate conversations. For example, a customer support bot for an e-commerce platform can retrieve details about order statuses or product availability from an external database.

B. Document Summarization

With RAG, NLP systems can retrieve relevant sections of a lengthy document and generate a concise summary. This is particularly useful in:

- Legal settings, where retrieving specific case laws is critical.
- Academic research, where summarizing lengthy papers is invaluable.

C. Personalized Recommendations

RAG enables NLP systems to retrieve user-specific data, enhancing personalized recommendations. For example:

- In **healthcare**, RAG can fetch patient history to offer tailored treatment suggestions.
- In **retail**, it can retrieve past purchases to recommend complementary products.

Real-World Applications of RAG

1. **Healthcare**

    - **Example:** A medical assistant that retrieves research papers to provide insights for doctors.

2. **E-commerce**

    - **Example:** Personalized shopping assistants that suggest products based on real-time trends and user preferences.

3. **Education**
   - **Example:** An AI tutor that retrieves relevant learning materials and generates explanations tailored to students' needs.

4. **Enterprise Search**
   - **Example:** Internal tools for organizations to find documents, emails, and other knowledge assets quickly.

Practical Exercise: Build a Simple RAG Workflow

This section will guide you through building a simple **Retrieval-Augmented Generation (RAG)** workflow. Using

Python, we will create a system that retrieves relevant information from a knowledge base and uses a generative model to produce accurate, context-aware responses. This project is suitable for both beginners and advanced users.

What We'll Build

We'll develop a system that performs the following tasks:

1. **Stores and indexes knowledge** for efficient retrieval.
2. **Retrieves relevant knowledge** based on a user's query.
3. **Generates responses** by combining the retrieved knowledge with a query using a language model.

This approach is applicable in real-world scenarios like customer support bots, question-answering systems, or personal assistants.

Step 1: Prerequisites

Using Python, ensure you have the following:

- Python 3.7 or later.
- Installed libraries: `transformers`, `sentence-transformers`, and `faiss-cpu`.

Install the required libraries by running:

`pip install transformers sentence-transformers faiss-cpu`

Step 2: Setting Up the Knowledge Base

We'll create a small knowledge base of information on climate change. This data will serve as the foundation for retrieval operations.

```python
# Step 1: Define a knowledge base as a list of strings
knowledge_base = [
    "Climate change refers to long-term changes in temperature and weather patterns.",
    "Burning fossil fuels is a major cause of global warming.",
    "Renewable energy sources like solar and wind help reduce greenhouse gas emissions.",
    "Deforestation contributes to an increase in carbon dioxide in the atmosphere.",
    "Rising sea levels are a direct consequence of melting polar ice caps."
]
```

This simple dataset will later be encoded and indexed for efficient retrieval.

Step 3: Encoding the Knowledge Base

Using Python, we'll use the `sentence-transformers` library to encode each entry in the knowledge base into numerical vectors, making them machine-readable for retrieval.

```
from sentence_transformers import SentenceTransformer

import numpy as np


# Load a pre-trained embedding model
embedding_model = SentenceTransformer('all-MiniLM-L6-v2')
```

```python
# Encode each knowledge base entry into a vector
embeddings = embedding_model.encode(knowledge_base)

print("Embeddings created for the knowledge base.")
```

Step 4: Creating a Searchable Index

Using Python and the FAISS library, we'll index these embeddings to allow quick and accurate retrieval of relevant information.

import faiss

Create a FAISS index for similarity search

dimension = embeddings[0].shape[0]   # Dimensionality of the embeddings

index = faiss.IndexFlatL2(dimension)   # L2 distance metric for similarity

index.add(np.array(embeddings))   # Add embeddings to the index

print(f"Knowledge base indexed with {index.ntotal} entries.")

Now, the knowledge base is indexed and ready for retrieval.

Step 5: Defining the Retrieval Function

Using Python, we'll implement a function that retrieves the most relevant entry from the knowledge base based on a query.

def retrieve_relevant_info(query, index, kb, model):

"""

Retrieve the most relevant fact from the knowledge base for a given query.

"""

Encode the query into a vector

query_embedding = model.encode([query])

Search the FAISS index for the closest match

```
    distances, indices = index.search(np.array(query_embedding), k=1)

    # Get the best match from the knowledge base
    retrieved_fact = kb[indices[0][0]]

    return retrieved_fact
```

This function takes a user query, encodes it into a numerical vector, and retrieves the most similar entry from the knowledge base.

Step 6: Integrating a Generative Model

Using Python and the Hugging Face `transformers` library, we'll incorporate a pre-trained generative model (e.g., **BART**) to generate responses.

```
from transformers import AutoTokenizer, AutoModelForSeq2SeqLM
```

Load the BART model and tokenizer

```
tokenizer = AutoTokenizer.from_pretrained("facebook/bart-large")

generation_model = AutoModelForSeq2SeqLM.from_pretrained("facebook/bart-large")


def generate_response(query, retrieved_fact):
    """
```

Generate a response using a generative model with retrieved context.
"""

Combine query and retrieved fact

context = f"Context: {retrieved_fact}\nQuestion: {query}"

Tokenize the input and generate a response

input_ids = tokenizer(context, return_tensors="pt").input_ids

output_ids = generation_model.generate(input_ids, max_length=50, num_beams=4, early_stopping=True)

```
    return
tokenizer.decode(output_ids[0],
skip_special_tokens=True)
```

Step 7: Building the Complete Workflow

Using Python, we'll combine retrieval and generation into a single workflow.

```
def rag_workflow(query):
    """
    End-to-end RAG workflow that
    retrieves relevant knowledge and
    generates a response.
    """
    # Step 1: Retrieve relevant information
    retrieved_fact = retrieve_relevant_info(query, index, knowledge_base, embedding_model)
```

```
# Step 2: Generate a response using the retrieved information

response = generate_response(query, retrieved_fact)


return retrieved_fact, response
```

Step 8: Testing the Workflow

Using Python, test the RAG pipeline with example queries.

```
# Example queries

queries = [

    "What is climate change?",
```

```
    "How can we reduce greenhouse gas emissions?",

    "What happens when forests are cut down?"

]


for query in queries:

    retrieved, response = rag_workflow(query)

    print(f"Query: {query}")

    print(f"Retrieved Fact: {retrieved}")

    print(f"Generated Response: {response}")

    print("-" * 50)
```

Expected Output

Query: What is climate change?

Retrieved Fact: Climate change refers to long-term changes in temperature and weather patterns.

Generated Response: Climate change refers to shifts in temperature and weather patterns over a long period.

Query: How can we reduce greenhouse gas emissions?

Retrieved Fact: Renewable energy sources like solar and wind help reduce greenhouse gas emissions.

Generated Response: Using renewable energy sources like solar and wind can significantly reduce emissions.

Query: What happens when forests are cut down?

Retrieved Fact: Deforestation contributes to an increase in carbon dioxide in the atmosphere.

Generated Response: Cutting down forests increases CO2 levels, worsening climate change effects.

Optional Enhancements

1. Extend the knowledge base with larger datasets (e.g., Wikipedia).
2. Experiment with different embedding models, such as OpenAI embeddings.
3. Build a user-friendly interface using frameworks like Flask or Streamlit.

Chapter 2: Understanding the Foundations

To build effective **Retrieval-Augmented Generation (RAG)** systems, it's essential to understand the core components that form its foundation. This chapter introduces the building blocks of RAG, focusing on the roles of large language models (LLMs), knowledge bases, and information retrieval. By the end, you'll grasp how RAG integrates these elements to deliver more powerful and contextually aware solutions.

2.1 Large Language Models (LLMs): Capabilities and Limitations

Large Language Models (LLMs) are one of the most transformative technologies in modern Natural Language Processing (NLP). These models, such as GPT, BERT, and T5, have advanced capabilities, including text generation, translation, summarization, and more. However, despite their impressive abilities, LLMs also have inherent limitations. This section explores what makes LLMs powerful, where they fall short, and how practitioners can effectively harness their potential.

Capabilities of LLMs

Large Language Models are trained on vast amounts of text data, enabling them to recognize patterns, relationships, and structures in language. Here are some key capabilities:

1. Natural Language Understanding

LLMs excel at parsing and interpreting human language. They can understand the intent behind user inputs and respond in meaningful ways. For example, an LLM can determine whether a question is asking for factual data or opinion-based information.

2. Contextual Text Generation

One of the standout features of LLMs is their ability to generate coherent, contextually relevant text. Whether writing a poem or drafting a business email, LLMs can produce outputs that often resemble human writing.

3. Few-Shot and Zero-Shot Learning

LLMs can perform tasks with minimal (few-shot) or no (zero-shot) specific examples. This flexibility is particularly useful when handling diverse NLP tasks.

4. Multilingual Capabilities

Many LLMs can work across multiple languages, making them valuable for global applications like translation services or cross-language search engines.

Example

A customer service chatbot powered by an LLM can handle diverse queries, such as troubleshooting, order tracking, or FAQs, while maintaining a conversational tone.

Limitations of LLMs

Despite their strengths, LLMs are not without flaws. Understanding these limitations is essential for designing robust systems:

1. Knowledge Cutoff

LLMs are trained on static datasets and cannot access real-time or updated information unless explicitly connected to a knowledge base. For instance, an LLM trained in 2022 would not know about events or developments from 2023 onward.

2. Hallucinations

LLMs sometimes generate information that is factually incorrect or nonsensical. This phenomenon, known as hallucination, can mislead users or produce unreliable outputs.

3. Context Management

Maintaining context over long conversations or documents can be challenging for LLMs, leading to irrelevant or repetitive responses.

4. Computational Cost

Training and deploying large-scale models require significant computational resources, making them inaccessible for smaller teams or organizations.

Practical Insight

For a task like summarizing news articles, an LLM might excel at providing a concise summary but fail to verify the accuracy of its content unless paired with a real-time data retrieval system.

Hands-On Exercise: Explore LLM Capabilities

In this exercise, we'll use **Python** and OpenAI's GPT model to experiment with the capabilities of an LLM. We'll test its ability to understand queries, generate coherent text, and handle multilingual input.

Setup

First, ensure you have the `openai` Python library installed. You can install it with:

```
pip install openai
```

Code Example: Querying GPT

Here's a Python script to interact with an LLM (e.g., OpenAI's GPT-3). Ensure you have an API key from OpenAI.

```python
import openai

# Set up your OpenAI API key
openai.api_key = "your-api-key-here"

# Define a function to query the LLM
def query_gpt(prompt, model="text-davinci-003", max_tokens=100):
    response = openai.Completion.create(
        engine=model,
```

```python
        prompt=prompt,
        max_tokens=max_tokens,
        temperature=0.7
    )
    return response.choices[0].text.strip()

# Test the LLM with a simple prompt
prompt = "Explain the significance of renewable energy in reducing climate change."
response = query_gpt(prompt)
print("LLM Response:\n", response)

# Test multilingual capabilities
prompt_multilingual = "Translate 'How are you?' to French."
```

```
response_multilingual = query_gpt(prompt_multilingual)

print("\nMultilingual Translation:\n", response_multilingual)
```

Expected Output

For the first query, the LLM might generate:

LLM Response:

Renewable energy is crucial in mitigating climate change as it reduces reliance on fossil fuels, lowering greenhouse gas emissions and promoting sustainability.

For the multilingual query:

Multilingual Translation:

Comment ça va ?

Mitigating LLM Limitations

To address the shortcomings of LLMs, practitioners often combine them with complementary tools and strategies:

1. Augmenting with Retrieval

Pairing LLMs with knowledge bases allows them to access real-time or domain-specific information, enhancing accuracy.

2. Fine-Tuning

Fine-tuning LLMs on domain-specific datasets can significantly improve their performance for specialized tasks.

3. Human-in-the-Loop

In critical applications like healthcare or legal systems, involving humans to verify outputs ensures reliability.

Practical Exercise: Fine-Tuning an LLM

For users interested in customization, this exercise explores how to fine-tune a pre-trained LLM on a specific dataset.

Procedure

1. Prepare your dataset in JSONL format, where each line is a training example with `prompt` and `completion`.
2. Use OpenAI's fine-tuning API to train the model.

Python Code for Fine-Tuning

```
# Assuming you have a JSONL file named 'fine_tune_data.jsonl'
```

```
# Upload the training file
openai.File.create(file=open("fine_tune_data.jsonl"), purpose="fine-tune")


# Start the fine-tuning process
fine_tune_job = openai.FineTune.create(training_file="file-id-here", model="curie")


# Monitor fine-tuning progress
print("Fine-Tuning Job ID:", fine_tune_job.id)


# Check fine-tuned model results
model_name = fine_tune_job["fine_tuned_model"]
```

```
response = query_gpt("Your specialized prompt here", model=model_name)

print("Fine-Tuned Model Response:\n", response)
```

2.2 Knowledge Bases: Structured, Unstructured, and Hybrid Approaches

Knowledge bases (KBs) play a crucial role in enhancing retrieval-augmented generation (RAG) workflows. They serve as the foundation for providing context, facts, and structured information that complements the generation capabilities of large language models (LLMs). In this chapter, we will break down the different types of knowledge bases, explore their characteristics, and see how they integrate into modern NLP workflows.

Structured Knowledge Bases

Structured knowledge bases organize information in predefined schemas, such as tables or graphs, making it easy to query specific facts. Examples include relational databases, knowledge graphs, and taxonomies.

Characteristics:

- Highly organized and easy to query.
- Ideal for representing relationships between entities.
- Examples: SQL databases, Wikidata, and Freebase.

Example: Wikidata

Wikidata is a free, structured knowledge base that organizes data about entities (like people, places, and events) in a graph structure. For example, you can query relationships like "Who is the president of a specific country?"

Using Python to Query a Structured KB (SPARQL and Wikidata)

We will use Python to demonstrate querying Wikidata using SPARQL, a query language for RDF (Resource Description Framework).

Using Python to query Wikidata with SPARQL

import requests

Define the SPARQL endpoint and query

SPARQL_ENDPOINT = "https://query.wikidata.org/sparql"

query = """

SELECT ?country ?president WHERE {

```
    ?country wdt:P31 wd:Q6256. # Entity type is a country

    ?country wdt:P6 ?president. # Entity has a president

    ?president rdfs:label ?presidentName.

    FILTER(LANG(?presidentName) = "en")
}
LIMIT 5
"""


# Send the query to the endpoint
response = requests.get(SPARQL_ENDPOINT, params={"query": query, "format": "json"})
data = response.json()


# Print the results
```

```
for item in data["results"]["bindings"]:
    print(f"Country: {item['country']['value']}, President: {item['president']['value']}")
```

Unstructured Knowledge Bases

Unstructured knowledge bases store data without predefined schemas. Examples include documents, PDFs, or entire websites. These are often processed using natural language processing techniques to extract relevant information.

Characteristics:

- Flexible and can store diverse content types.
- Data retrieval relies on NLP techniques.

- Examples: Wikipedia, research papers, and raw text corpora.

Example: Wikipedia as an Unstructured KB

Wikipedia serves as an excellent example of an unstructured KB. Since articles are in plain text, search engines or NLP models are used to extract specific facts.

Using Python to Extract Information from Wikipedia

We'll use the Python library `wikipedia-api` to extract information from Wikipedia.

Using Python to retrieve data from Wikipedia

import wikipediaapi

Initialize the Wikipedia API

```python
wiki = wikipediaapi.Wikipedia("en")

# Fetch an article
page = wiki.page("Natural_language_processing")

if page.exists():
    print(f"Title: {page.title}")
    print(f"Summary: {page.summary[:500]}")  # Print the first 500 characters of the summary
else:
    print("Page not found.")
```

Hybrid Knowledge Bases

Hybrid KBs combine the best of structured and unstructured approaches. They include structured data for high-precision queries and unstructured data for broader context.

Characteristics:

- Flexible and scalable for diverse use cases.
- Examples: Enterprise knowledge graphs that integrate databases and document storage systems.

Example: Google Knowledge Graph

Google's Knowledge Graph is a hybrid system that combines structured data (entity relationships) with unstructured web content to enhance search results.

Exercise: Create a Simple KB Workflow

Objective: Create a hybrid KB workflow that queries structured data from a CSV and unstructured data from plain text.

Using Python to Implement a Simple KB Workflow

1. **Structured Data**: We'll load and query a CSV file containing country and president data.
2. **Unstructured Data**: We'll query Wikipedia for additional details about each president.

Using Python to create a hybrid KB workflow

import pandas as pd

import wikipediaapi

```python
# Load structured data from a CSV
data = {
    "Country": ["USA", "France", "Germany"],
    "President": ["Joe Biden", "Emmanuel Macron", "Frank-Walter Steinmeier"]
}
df = pd.DataFrame(data)


# Initialize Wikipedia API for unstructured data
wiki = wikipediaapi.Wikipedia("en")


# Function to fetch additional details from Wikipedia
def get_wikipedia_summary(name):
    page = wiki.page(name)
```

```python
    return page.summary[:200] if page.exists() else "No information available."

# Query both structured and unstructured data
for index, row in df.iterrows():
    country = row["Country"]
    president = row["President"]
    print(f"Country: {country}")
    print(f"President: {president}")
    print("Additional Details:", get_wikipedia_summary(president))
    print("-" * 40)
```

Key Takeaways

- Structured KBs are efficient for precise queries but lack flexibility.
- Unstructured KBs offer flexibility but require NLP tools for effective retrieval.
- Hybrid KBs combine structured precision with unstructured breadth, making them ideal for RAG workflows.

By understanding these types of knowledge bases and their integration into RAG, you can design workflows that effectively leverage both structured data and free-form text to create more dynamic and informative NLP applications.

2.3 Fundamentals of Information Retrieval

Information retrieval (IR) forms the backbone of retrieval-augmented generation (RAG) systems. It's the process of finding relevant information in a collection of unstructured or structured data. Whether you're searching for a document, a snippet of text, or specific facts, IR helps you efficiently locate what you need. This chapter explores the core concepts of IR, focusing on its relevance to modern natural language processing (NLP).

What is Information Retrieval?

Information retrieval involves retrieving documents, passages, or data that satisfy a user query from a collection of resources.

Key Components of IR

1. **Corpus**: The collection of documents or data.
2. **Query**: The user's request for information (e.g., keywords or questions).
3. **Indexing**: Organizing the corpus for faster searching.
4. **Ranking**: Ordering search results based on relevance.

Sparse vs. Dense Retrieval

IR methods are broadly categorized into **sparse** and **dense** retrieval approaches.

Sparse Retrieval

Sparse retrieval relies on term-matching techniques, such as TF-IDF and BM25, where relevance is based on matching keywords between a query and a document.

- **Advantages**: Fast, interpretable, and computationally inexpensive.
- **Disadvantages**: Limited understanding of synonyms or semantic meaning.

Dense Retrieval

Dense retrieval uses embeddings—numerical vector representations of text. Neural networks generate these embeddings, capturing the semantic meaning of words and sentences.

- **Advantages**: Captures deeper meanings, supports synonyms, and handles complex queries.
- **Disadvantages**: Requires more computational resources and training data.

Sparse Retrieval Example: TF-IDF and BM25

TF-IDF (Term Frequency-Inverse Document Frequency) is a scoring model that evaluates how relevant a word is to a document relative to a corpus.

BM25, an extension of TF-IDF, is a ranking function widely used in search engines.

Using Python to Implement Sparse Retrieval

We will use Python's `scikit-learn` library to compute TF-IDF and rank documents based on a query.

Using Python for sparse retrieval with TF-IDF

from sklearn.feature_extraction.text import TfidfVectorizer

from sklearn.metrics.pairwise import cosine_similarity

```python
# Sample corpus
corpus = [
    "Information retrieval is key to NLP.",
    "TF-IDF is a sparse retrieval method.",
    "Dense retrieval uses embeddings for better understanding."
]

# Query
query = "retrieval NLP"

# Create TF-IDF vectors
vectorizer = TfidfVectorizer()
```

```
tfidf_matrix = vectorizer.fit_transform(corpus + [query])

# Compute cosine similarity between query and documents
similarities = cosine_similarity(tfidf_matrix[-1], tfidf_matrix[:-1])

# Display results
for idx, score in enumerate(similarities[0]):
    print(f"Document {idx + 1}: {corpus[idx]}")
    print(f"Similarity Score: {score:.2f}")
    print("-" * 40)
```

Dense Retrieval Example: Sentence Transformers

Dense retrieval uses embeddings to capture semantic relationships. Sentence embeddings can be created using pre-trained models like `sentence-transformers` in Python.

Using Python to Implement Dense Retrieval

\# Using Python for dense retrieval with Sentence Transformers

from sentence_transformers import SentenceTransformer, util

\# Load a pre-trained model

model = SentenceTransformer('all-MiniLM-L6-v2')

```python
# Sample corpus
corpus = [
    "Information retrieval is key to NLP.",
    "TF-IDF is a sparse retrieval method.",
    "Dense retrieval uses embeddings for better understanding."
]

# Query
query = "retrieval in natural language processing"

# Generate embeddings for the corpus and query
```

```python
corpus_embeddings = model.encode(corpus, convert_to_tensor=True)

query_embedding = model.encode(query, convert_to_tensor=True)


# Compute similarity scores
similarities = util.pytorch_cos_sim(query_embedding, corpus_embeddings)


# Display results
for idx, score in enumerate(similarities[0]):
    print(f"Document {idx + 1}: {corpus[idx]}")
    print(f"Similarity Score: {score:.2f}")
```

```
print("-" * 40)
```

Key Considerations in IR for RAG

1. **Efficiency**: Sparse methods are computationally faster for large datasets, while dense methods require more resources but are semantically richer.
2. **Scalability**: Indexing large corpora efficiently is critical for real-time retrieval.
3. **Hybrid Approaches**: Combining sparse and dense retrieval often yields better results, leveraging the strengths of both.

Exercise: Implement a Hybrid IR Workflow

Objective: Combine sparse (TF-IDF) and dense retrieval methods for better search results.

Using Python for a hybrid IR workflow

from sklearn.feature_extraction.text import TfidfVectorizer

from sentence_transformers import SentenceTransformer, util

import numpy as np

Sample corpus

corpus = [

   "Information retrieval is key to NLP.",

   "TF-IDF is a sparse retrieval method.",

"Dense retrieval uses embeddings for better understanding."

]

Query

query = "retrieval in natural language processing"

Step 1: Sparse Retrieval with TF-IDF

tfidf_vectorizer = TfidfVectorizer()

tfidf_matrix = tfidf_vectorizer.fit_transform(corpus + [query])

tfidf_scores = cosine_similarity(tfidf_matrix[-1], tfidf_matrix[:-1])[0]

```python
# Step 2: Dense Retrieval with Sentence Transformers
dense_model = SentenceTransformer('all-MiniLM-L6-v2')
corpus_embeddings = dense_model.encode(corpus, convert_to_tensor=True)
query_embedding = dense_model.encode(query, convert_to_tensor=True)
dense_scores = util.pytorch_cos_sim(query_embedding, corpus_embeddings)[0].numpy()


# Step 3: Combine Scores
combined_scores = (0.5 * tfidf_scores) + (0.5 * dense_scores)
```

```
# Display Results
for idx, score in enumerate(combined_scores):
    print(f"Document {idx + 1}: {corpus[idx]}")
    print(f"Combined Score: {score:.2f}")
    print("-" * 40)
```

Key Takeaways

- Sparse and dense retrieval methods have distinct strengths.
- Dense retrieval excels in semantic understanding but is computationally intensive.
- Combining sparse and dense methods in a hybrid workflow provides robust and precise results.

This understanding of IR fundamentals will be your foundation for building effective RAG systems, whether you're retrieving structured knowledge or processing unstructured data.

2.4 How RAG Combines Retrieval and Generation

Retrieval-Augmented Generation (RAG) bridges the gap between searching for relevant information and generating contextually accurate responses. By combining retrieval mechanisms with generative models, RAG systems provide detailed, relevant, and dynamic answers to user queries, even when the query involves complex or niche topics.

This chapter explores the synergy between retrieval and generation, breaking down the workflow and demonstrating how retrieval and generation come together to form the backbone of RAG systems.

The Two Components of RAG

RAG works by integrating two critical components:

1. **Retrieval**

    - Finds relevant context or knowledge from a data source.
    - Uses either sparse or dense retrieval (discussed earlier).

2. **Generation**

    - Produces coherent, human-like text based on the retrieved context.
    - Utilizes language models like GPT, T5, or BERT.

The retrieval step ensures the generative model has access to factual and contextually relevant knowledge, addressing limitations of language models that rely solely on static training data.

How RAG Works

1. **Query Input**: A user submits a query (e.g., "What are the benefits of solar energy?").
2. **Retrieve**: The system searches a knowledge base for relevant documents or passages.
3. **Generate**: A language model uses the retrieved information to generate an answer.

This combination ensures responses are both accurate and contextually rich.

Key Advantages of RAG

- **Dynamic Updates**: Retrieves up-to-date information, avoiding the static nature of traditional language models.
- **Fact-Aware Responses**: Reduces hallucinations by grounding answers in factual sources.
- **Versatility**: Combines structured and unstructured knowledge retrieval for complex scenarios.

Workflow of a RAG System

Step 1: Retrieving Context

The retrieval system fetches relevant information from a predefined corpus, using sparse or dense retrieval techniques.

Step 2: Conditioning the Generator

The retrieved context is passed as input to the generative model, enabling it to produce context-aware responses.

Step 3: Generating the Response

The generative model processes both the query and the retrieved context to produce a final output.

Building a RAG Workflow: Practical Exercise

In this exercise, we'll build a basic RAG workflow using Python, OpenAI's `GPT` for generation, and `Sentence-Transformers` for dense retrieval.

Step 1: Install Required Libraries

Make sure you have the following libraries installed:

pip install openai sentence-transformers faiss-cpu

Step 2: Implementing the RAG Workflow

Using Python for the RAG workflow

Step 1: Import Libraries

from sentence_transformers import SentenceTransformer, util

import openai

import numpy as np

Step 2: Initialize Models

```python
# Load a pre-trained dense retrieval model
retrieval_model = SentenceTransformer('all-MiniLM-L6-v2')

# Set OpenAI API key
openai.api_key = 'your_openai_api_key'

# Step 3: Define Corpus (Knowledge Base)
corpus = [
    "Solar energy is renewable and environmentally friendly.",
    "Solar panels convert sunlight into electricity using photovoltaic cells.",
    "The use of solar energy reduces carbon emissions significantly.",
```

    "Solar energy systems can lower electricity bills."

]

Encode corpus to dense embeddings

corpus_embeddings = retrieval_model.encode(corpus, convert_to_tensor=True)

Step 4: Define User Query

query = "What are the benefits of solar energy?"

Encode query to dense embedding

query_embedding = retrieval_model.encode(query, convert_to_tensor=True)

```python
# Step 5: Retrieve Relevant Documents

# Compute cosine similarity scores
similarities = util.pytorch_cos_sim(query_embedding, corpus_embeddings)

top_k = 2  # Retrieve top 2 relevant documents
top_results = torch.topk(similarities, k=top_k)


retrieved_context = []
for idx in top_results.indices[0]:
    retrieved_context.append(corpus[idx])


# Step 6: Generate Response
```

```python
# Prepare prompt for the generative model
prompt = (
    f"Answer the following question based on the context provided:\n\n"
    f"Context: {' '.join(retrieved_context)}\n\n"
    f"Question: {query}\n\n"
    f"Answer:"
)

# Call OpenAI GPT API to generate a response
response = openai.Completion.create(
    engine="text-davinci-003",
    prompt=prompt,
    max_tokens=100
```

)

Step 7: Display Results

print("Query:", query)

print("Retrieved Context:", retrieved_context)

print("Generated Answer:", response['choices'][0]['text'].strip())

Code Walkthrough

1. **Retrieval Model**: We use `SentenceTransformer` to encode both the query and the knowledge base into dense embeddings.
2. **Similarity Scoring**: The system retrieves the top-k most similar documents using cosine similarity.

3. **Prompt Design**: The retrieved documents are passed to GPT as context for generation.
4. **Response Generation**: GPT generates a human-like answer grounded in the retrieved knowledge.

Advanced Enhancements

1. **Multi-Hop Retrieval**: For complex queries, retrieve additional layers of context by chaining retrieval and generation steps.
2. **Hybrid Systems**: Combine sparse and dense retrieval for improved relevance.
3. **Knowledge Base Updates**: Periodically update the corpus to keep the system dynamic and current.

Example

A customer support chatbot uses RAG to provide answers. When asked about a product feature, the chatbot retrieves documentation and combines it with a pre-trained language model to offer a detailed response.

- **Query**: "What is the warranty period for Product X?"
- **Retrieved Context**: "Product X has a 12-month warranty period covering manufacturing defects."
- **Generated Answer**: "Product X comes with a 12-month warranty that covers any manufacturing defects. For more details, refer to the warranty documentation."

Key Takeaways

- RAG combines the precision of retrieval with the versatility of generation.
- By grounding generation in retrieved context, RAG mitigates hallucination issues.
- Practical applications include chatbots, search engines, and question-answering systems.

Mastering RAG will allow you to build systems that are both intelligent and reliable, capable of adapting to dynamic data environments.

Chapter 3. Getting Started with RAG

Retrieval-Augmented Generation (RAG) systems can seem daunting at first, but this chapter simplifies the process of getting started. We'll explore the tools, libraries, and frameworks necessary for RAG development, guide you through installation and configuration, and walk you through creating your first RAG workflow.

3.1 Tools and Libraries for RAG Development

Retrieval-Augmented Generation (RAG) is built on a rich ecosystem of tools and libraries. These tools handle critical aspects of retrieval, language generation, and orchestration, enabling developers to combine state-of-the-art machine learning techniques with efficient system design. This section introduces essential tools for developing RAG systems, explaining their roles and how they integrate seamlessly into your workflow.

Key Tools for RAG Development

1. Python

Python serves as the backbone for RAG development due to its vast ecosystem, simplicity, and community support. Its extensive libraries for machine learning, natural language processing, and system integration make it the go-to choice for most developers.

2. FAISS

Facebook AI Similarity Search (FAISS) is a library designed for efficient similarity search and clustering of dense vectors. It's perfect for dense retrieval tasks where high-speed similarity matching is required.

- **Use Case**: Retrieve semantically similar documents or embeddings.
- **Why FAISS?**: It's optimized for both memory efficiency and speed, enabling scalable retrieval.

3. ElasticSearch

ElasticSearch is a robust, open-source search engine known for its ability to handle large datasets for sparse retrieval. It excels at performing keyword-based searches over unstructured text.

- **Use Case**: Perform text-based queries to retrieve information from large, unstructured datasets.
- **Why ElasticSearch?**: It offers fast indexing, a powerful query language, and integration with other tools.

4. LangChain

LangChain simplifies building systems that combine language models with external data and tools. It provides prebuilt modules for chaining together different components of RAG workflows, such as retrieval, prompting, and generation.

- **Use Case**: Develop pipelines to combine retrieval and generation seamlessly.
- **Why LangChain?**: It abstracts much of the boilerplate code, allowing developers to focus on high-level logic.

5. Pretrained LLMs

Pretrained large language models are the cornerstone of RAG systems. Popular options include:

- **OpenAI GPT Models**: Known for their fluency and accuracy in

generating natural language responses.
- **Hugging Face Models**: Offers a variety of open-source models, such as T5, BERT, and GPT-like architectures, catering to diverse use cases.

Integrating Tools into Your Workflow

Each tool complements the others in building a complete RAG system. Here's how they fit together:

- **FAISS** handles dense retrieval by comparing query vectors with precomputed document embeddings.
- **ElasticSearch** serves as a keyword-based search tool for sparse retrieval tasks.
- **LangChain** ties everything together, making it easy to pass

data between retrieval and generation components.
- **Pretrained LLMs** process the retrieved data and generate human-like responses.

Hands-On: Installing These Tools

Before diving into implementation, let's install the required tools. Make sure you have Python 3.8 or later installed on your system.

Step 1: Set Up a Virtual Environment

Using a virtual environment ensures your dependencies are isolated from other projects.

Install virtualenv if not already installed

pip install virtualenv

Create and activate a virtual environment

virtualenv rag_env

source rag_env/bin/activate   # For Mac/Linux

rag_env\Scripts\activate   # For Windows

Step 2: Install Required Libraries

Now, install the libraries you'll use in your RAG workflow:

Install FAISS

pip install faiss-cpu

Install ElasticSearch Python client

pip install elasticsearch

```
# Install LangChain
pip install langchain

# Install Hugging Face Transformers
pip install transformers

# Install OpenAI API client
pip install openai
```

Example: Using FAISS for Dense Retrieval

Let's see FAISS in action. Here, we'll create a simple dense retrieval system.

Using Python to Build the Example

```python
# Import necessary libraries

import faiss

import numpy as np


# Step 1: Define a knowledge base (dense vectors)

knowledge_base = np.random.random((5, 128)).astype('float32')   # Example 5 vectors of 128 dimensions


# Step 2: Build the FAISS index

index = faiss.IndexFlatL2(128)   # L2 (Euclidean) distance for similarity search

index.add(knowledge_base)   # Add vectors to the index
```

Step 3: Define a query vector

query_vector = np.random.random((1, 128)).astype('float32')

Step 4: Perform the search

k = 3 # Retrieve top 3 results

distances, indices = index.search(query_vector, k)

Step 5: Display results

print("Query Vector:", query_vector)

print("Nearest Neighbors Indices:", indices)

print("Distances:", distances)

Explanation of the Code

- **Knowledge Base**: Represents stored information as dense vectors. In real-world applications, these would be embeddings of documents.
- **FAISS Index**: Built to quickly search for similar vectors.
- **Query Vector**: Represents the user query, also in dense vector format.
- **Results**: Indices and distances of the closest vectors in the knowledge base to the query.

Next Steps

The tools and libraries covered in this section form the foundation of RAG development. In the upcoming sections, we'll configure these tools further, integrate them into workflows, and create a fully functional RAG system.

With these tools in your toolkit, you're equipped to start building intelligent systems that retrieve and generate knowledge-rich responses.

3.2 Installing and Configuring Python, FAISS, LangChain, and ElasticSearch

To get started with building a Retrieval-Augmented Generation (RAG) system, setting up the right tools and libraries is essential. This chapter walks you through the step-by-step process of installing and configuring Python, FAISS, LangChain, and ElasticSearch. By the end of this section, you'll have a fully operational environment to start building your RAG workflows.

Prerequisites

Before we dive in, ensure you have the following installed on your system:

- **Python 3.8 or later**: Check by running `python --version` in your terminal.
- **pip**: Python's package manager. It typically comes bundled with Python.

Step 1: Install Python

If Python is not already installed, download and install it from the official [Python website](). During installation, ensure you check the box to **add Python to PATH**.

Setting Up the Environment

1. Create a Virtual Environment

Using a virtual environment isolates your project dependencies, preventing conflicts with other Python projects on your system.

```
# Install virtualenv if it's not already installed
pip install virtualenv


# Create a new virtual environment
virtualenv rag_env


# Activate the virtual environment
source rag_env/bin/activate   # For Mac/Linux
```

rag_env\Scripts\activate   # For Windows

Installing FAISS

FAISS is critical for dense vector retrieval. Its installation depends on whether you want CPU or GPU support.

Installing FAISS for CPU

pip install faiss-cpu

Installing FAISS for GPU

If you have a CUDA-enabled GPU and want to leverage its power for faster computation:

pip install faiss-gpu

Test the Installation

Using Python, run the following script to verify the installation:

Import the FAISS library

import faiss

Verify FAISS version

print("FAISS version:", faiss.__version__)

If the version prints successfully, FAISS is installed correctly.

Installing LangChain

LangChain simplifies building RAG workflows by chaining together retrieval and generation components.

pip install langchain

Verify LangChain Installation

Run this snippet to check if LangChain is installed properly:

Import LangChain

from langchain.chains import RetrievalQA

print("LangChain is ready to use!")

Installing and Configuring ElasticSearch

ElasticSearch is a robust search engine used for sparse retrieval. Setting it up involves installing the ElasticSearch server and its Python client.

Step 1: Download ElasticSearch

1. Visit the [ElasticSearch downloads page](#) and download the version compatible with your system.
2. Extract the downloaded file to a directory.

Step 2: Start the ElasticSearch Server

Navigate to the extracted directory and run:

For Mac/Linux

bin/elasticsearch

For Windows

bin\elasticsearch.bat

The server runs on `http://localhost:9200` by default.

Step 3: Install ElasticSearch Python Client

In your Python environment, install the client:

pip install elasticsearch

Verify ElasticSearch Installation

Using Python, check if the server and client are communicating:

from elasticsearch import Elasticsearch

Connect to the ElasticSearch server

```
es = Elasticsearch([{'host': 'localhost', 'port': 9200}])

# Check connection

if es.ping():

    print("ElasticSearch server is running!")

else:

    print("Failed to connect to ElasticSearch.")
```

Practical Exercise: Configuring a FAISS and ElasticSearch Hybrid Setup

Let's combine FAISS and ElasticSearch to set up a basic retrieval system.

Using Python

```python
from elasticsearch import Elasticsearch
import faiss
import numpy as np


# Step 1: Connect to ElasticSearch
es = Elasticsearch([{'host': 'localhost', 'port': 9200}])
if not es.ping():
    raise ValueError("ElasticSearch connection failed!")


# Step 2: Create an example FAISS index
dimension = 128  # Vector dimension
```

```python
faiss_index = faiss.IndexFlatL2(dimension)

# Step 3: Add dummy data to the FAISS index
# Example: 10 random vectors of 128 dimensions
dummy_vectors = np.random.random((10, dimension)).astype('float32')

faiss_index.add(dummy_vectors)

# Step 4: Perform a search in FAISS
query_vector = np.random.random((1, dimension)).astype('float32')

distances, indices = faiss_index.search(query_vector, k=3)  # Top 3 results
```

```
print("FAISS Results:")
for i, idx in enumerate(indices[0]):
    print(f"Vector Index: {idx}, Distance: {distances[0][i]}")


# Step 5: Store results in ElasticSearch
for idx in indices[0]:
    es.index(index='faiss_results', document={'vector_index': int(idx), 'distance': float(distances[0][idx])})


print("Results successfully stored in ElasticSearch.")
```

Key Takeaways

1. **FAISS and ElasticSearch Integration**: This setup provides a hybrid approach where dense and sparse retrieval methods complement each other.
2. **Virtual Environments**: Always use isolated environments for project-specific dependencies.
3. **LangChain**: It will simplify the orchestration of RAG workflows as we proceed in the next sections.

3.3 Setting Up Pretrained LLMs (OpenAI, Hugging Face, etc.)

Large Language Models (LLMs) such as those from OpenAI or Hugging Face form the backbone of Retrieval-Augmented Generation (RAG). In this chapter, we'll guide you step-by-step on setting up and using these pretrained models effectively. This includes installation, configuration, and usage tips for both beginners and experts.

Understanding Pretrained LLMs

Pretrained LLMs are language models trained on massive datasets to understand and generate human-like text. Popular platforms providing these models include:

- **OpenAI:** Known for GPT-3.5, GPT-4, and beyond, OpenAI offers highly capable models via APIs.
- **Hugging Face Transformers:** Provides a wide variety of open-source LLMs like BERT, GPT-2, and T5.

Each has its own strengths, and selecting the right model depends on your specific application.

Step 1: Installing Necessary Libraries

Before using any LLM, ensure your environment is equipped with the required libraries.

Using Python for Setup

We'll use Python, a widely adopted programming language for machine learning and natural language processing.

Install Hugging Face Transformers and OpenAI SDK:

Open a terminal and run:

pip install transformers openai

1.

Install Additional Libraries: For smooth execution, we also need libraries like `torch` (for Hugging Face models) and `dotenv` (for managing API keys securely):

pip install torch python-dotenv

2.

Step 2: Setting Up OpenAI API

The OpenAI API gives access to their cutting-edge models like GPT-3.5 and GPT-4.

1. **Obtain an API Key:**

    - Visit the [OpenAI website](#).
    - Sign in or create an account.
    - Navigate to the API keys section and generate a key.

Store the API Key Securely: Create a `.env` file in your project directory:

OPENAI_API_KEY=your_api_key_here

2.

Load the API Key in Python:

from dotenv import load_dotenv

import os

import openai

Load API key from .env file

load_dotenv()

openai.api_key = os.getenv("OPENAI_API_KEY")

Test the connection

response = openai.Completion.create(

   model="text-davinci-003",

    prompt="Hello, how are you?",

    max_tokens=10

)

print(response.choices[0].text.strip())

   3. This code initializes the API and tests it with a simple prompt.

Step 3: Setting Up Hugging Face Models

Hugging Face offers a diverse range of models, many of which are open-source.

Download and Use a Pretrained Model: The Hugging Face `transformers` library provides simple methods to load and use models. Below is an example of loading `GPT-2` for text generation:

```python
from transformers import GPT2LMHeadModel, GPT2Tokenizer

# Load tokenizer and model
tokenizer = GPT2Tokenizer.from_pretrained("gpt2")
model = GPT2LMHeadModel.from_pretrained("gpt2")

# Encode input text
input_text = "What is Retrieval-Augmented Generation?"
inputs = tokenizer.encode(input_text, return_tensors="pt")

# Generate output
```

```
outputs = model.generate(inputs, max_length=50, num_return_sequences=1, temperature=0.7)
```

```
# Decode and print the result
```

```
print(tokenizer.decode(outputs[0], skip_special_tokens=True))
```

1.
2. **Explore Other Models:** Hugging Face supports other types of models such as T5 for text-to-text tasks and BERT for embedding generation. You can explore the model hub at Hugging Face Models.

Practical Exercise: Switching Between OpenAI and Hugging Face Models

Let's create a script that dynamically selects between OpenAI and Hugging Face models based on user input.

Install Required Libraries:

pip install openai transformers torch python-dotenv

1.

Write the Python Script:

from transformers import GPT2LMHeadModel, GPT2Tokenizer

from dotenv import load_dotenv

import openai

import os

```python
# Load OpenAI API Key
load_dotenv()
openai.api_key = os.getenv("OPENAI_API_KEY")


def use_openai(prompt):
    response = openai.Completion.create(
        model="text-davinci-003",
        prompt=prompt,
        max_tokens=50
    )
    return response.choices[0].text.strip()


def use_huggingface(prompt):
```

```
    tokenizer = GPT2Tokenizer.from_pretrained("gpt2")

    model = GPT2LMHeadModel.from_pretrained("gpt2")

    inputs = tokenizer.encode(prompt, return_tensors="pt")

    outputs = model.generate(inputs, max_length=50, temperature=0.7)

    return tokenizer.decode(outputs[0], skip_special_tokens=True)


# User Input

print("Choose a model: 1) OpenAI 2) Hugging Face")

choice = input("Enter 1 or 2: ")
```

```
prompt = "Explain the concept of RAG."

if choice == "1":

    print("Using OpenAI:")

    print(use_openai(prompt))

elif choice == "2":

    print("Using Hugging Face:")

    print(use_huggingface(prompt))

else:

    print("Invalid choice.")
```

2.
3. **Run and Test:** Execute the script, choose the desired model, and observe the results.

Key Considerations When Setting Up LLMs

1. **Choose the Right Model:** Consider your use case. OpenAI models often excel in nuanced tasks, while Hugging Face provides flexibility and cost-efficiency.
2. **Fine-Tuning:** If out-of-the-box performance isn't sufficient, explore fine-tuning options, especially with Hugging Face models.
3. **Resource Management:** OpenAI API calls are billed per usage, while running Hugging Face models requires computational resources (GPU recommended).

By completing this section, you're now equipped to set up and use pretrained LLMs. In the next section, we'll bring everything together to create your first RAG workflow.

3.4 Creating Your First RAG Workflow

In this chapter, we will guide you through the process of creating your first **Retrieval-Augmented Generation (RAG)** workflow. RAG combines the power of retrieving knowledge from external sources with the ability of Large Language Models (LLMs) to generate coherent and context-aware responses. This is particularly useful when your LLM needs to provide domain-specific answers or handle scenarios requiring factual accuracy.

Step 1: Understanding the Workflow

A typical RAG workflow has the following components:

1. **Query Input:** The user's input that initiates the workflow.
2. **Retriever:** Searches for relevant information (e.g., documents or embeddings).
3. **Generator:** Uses the retrieved data to create a comprehensive response.
4. **Output:** Returns the final response to the user.

Step 2: Setting Up Your Environment

Before we start coding, let's set up the necessary tools and libraries.

Using Python for the Workflow

Ensure you have the following libraries installed. Open a terminal and run:

```
pip install openai langchain faiss-cpu python-dotenv
```

Step 3: Workflow Architecture

We'll create a Python script to:

1. Retrieve documents using FAISS.
2. Process the documents with LangChain.
3. Use an OpenAI model for response generation.

Here's how we'll do it.

Step 4: Step-by-Step Implementation

1. Set Up Your Environment Variables

We'll use `.env` to manage sensitive keys. Create a file named `.env` in your project directory:

OPENAI_API_KEY=your_openai_api_key

2. Create a Python Script

Let's walk through the entire workflow with a fully functional script.

\# Import required libraries

from langchain.vectorstores import FAISS

from langchain.embeddings.openai import OpenAIEmbeddings

```python
from langchain.chains import RetrievalQA

from langchain.prompts import PromptTemplate

from dotenv import load_dotenv

import openai

import os


# Load API key from .env file

load_dotenv()

openai.api_key = os.getenv("OPENAI_API_KEY")


# Step 1: Create a Sample Knowledge Base
```

```python
# Replace this with your actual data source

documents = [
    {"id": 1, "content": "RAG is a framework that combines retrieval and generation for better AI performance."},
    {"id": 2, "content": "FAISS is a library for efficient similarity search and clustering of dense vectors."},
    {"id": 3, "content": "LangChain simplifies the development of applications using LLMs."}
]


# Convert documents into embeddings using OpenAI
def create_embeddings(documents):
    embeddings = OpenAIEmbeddings()
```

```
    texts = [doc["content"] for doc in documents]

    return FAISS.from_texts(texts, embeddings)
```

Initialize FAISS with documents

```
print("Creating vector database...")
vector_db = create_embeddings(documents)
```

Step 2: Build the RAG Workflow

Define a custom prompt for the LLM

```
prompt_template = """
```

You are a helpful assistant. Use the following retrieved documents to answer the question:

```
{context}

Question: {question}

Answer:
"""

# Create a retrieval-based QA chain
retriever = vector_db.as_retriever()
qa_chain = RetrievalQA.from_chain_type(
    llm=openai.Completion.create,
    chain_type="stuff",
    retriever=retriever,
    chain_type_kwargs={"prompt_template": PromptTemplate(template=prompt_tem
```

```
    plate,        input_variables=["context", "question"])}
)

# Step 3: Handle User Query
def rag_query(question):
    return qa_chain.run(question)

# Test the RAG workflow
print("RAG Workflow Ready. Testing...")
user_query = "What is FAISS?"
response = rag_query(user_query)
print("Response:", response)
```

Step 5: Explanation of the Code

1. **Create the Knowledge Base:**

   - We manually define a small dataset of documents for simplicity.
   - Each document is transformed into dense vector embeddings using OpenAI's embeddings API.

2. **Initialize FAISS:**

   - FAISS indexes the document vectors to enable fast similarity searches.

3. **Build the RAG Workflow:**

   - The retriever searches for relevant documents.

- A custom prompt instructs the LLM to use retrieved data for response generation.

4. **Query the System:**

    - The user provides a question (e.g., "What is FAISS?"), and the system retrieves relevant information and generates an answer.

Practical Exercise: Enhance the Workflow

Let's extend the workflow to handle more complex queries by incorporating more documents and tweaking the prompt.

1. **Add More Documents:** Update the `documents` list with diverse content to enhance the system's versatility.

2. **Fine-Tune the Prompt:** Modify the `prompt_template` to encourage more detailed or concise answers based on your application.

Real-World Example: Customer Support Chatbot

A RAG workflow can be applied to build a customer support chatbot:

1. **Knowledge Base:** Use product manuals and FAQs as the source data.
2. **Retriever:** FAISS retrieves relevant sections of the knowledge base.
3. **Generator:** The LLM crafts personalized responses based on the retrieved content.

customer_query = "How can I reset my account password?"

```
response = rag_query(customer_query)

print("Customer Support Response:", response)
```

Tips for Scaling the Workflow

1. **Leverage Larger Models:** Use models like GPT-4 for nuanced responses.
2. **Optimize the Retriever:** Experiment with other vector databases like Pinecone or Weaviate for specific use cases.
3. **Automate Updates:** Regularly refresh the knowledge base with new data to keep the system accurate.

By following this guide, you've built your first RAG workflow! This foundational workflow can be expanded and adapted for various use cases, from customer support systems to personalized education platforms. In the next chapter, we'll delve into optimizing retrieval techniques to maximize the efficiency of your RAG workflows.

Chapter 4. Building the RAG Architecture

Retrieval-Augmented Generation (RAG) is built upon a structured architecture that integrates information retrieval with generative modeling. This chapter breaks down the components, processes, and optimization strategies for implementing a robust RAG pipeline. Whether you're a beginner or an expert, you'll find clear explanations, hands-on tutorials, and practical examples to guide you.

4.1 The Two-Stage Pipeline: Retriever and Generator Explained

The foundation of Retrieval-Augmented Generation (RAG) lies in its **two-stage pipeline**: the **Retriever** and the **Generator**. This modular design combines the strengths of both retrieval systems and language models, creating a powerful mechanism for generating informed, context-aware responses.

Let's dive into each component, understand its role, and learn how they work together.

The Role of the Retriever

The **retriever** is responsible for fetching relevant pieces of information from a pre-defined knowledge base. Its job is to filter out noise and surface only the most relevant data, which will help the generator create meaningful outputs.

Key Characteristics of the Retriever:

- **Focus on Relevance**: Retrieves data based on its proximity to the input query.

- **Efficiency**: Reduces the scope of data the generator has to process, speeding up response times.
- **Scalability**: Can handle large datasets using efficient indexing techniques.

A common example of a retriever in RAG workflows is **FAISS**, a high-performance library for similarity search and clustering of dense vectors.

The Role of the Generator

The **generator** is a language model tasked with creating responses that are not only accurate but also contextually coherent. It takes the data retrieved by the retriever, combines it with the user's query, and crafts a well-informed response.

Key Characteristics of the Generator:

- **Context Awareness**: Produces responses that incorporate retrieved information.
- **Flexibility**: Can adapt to various types of queries and domains.
- **Generative Power**: Fills in gaps and rephrases content for natural language outputs.

Pretrained language models like **OpenAI's GPT** and **Hugging Face Transformers** are commonly used as generators.

How They Work Together

The retriever and generator work in tandem to provide accurate and meaningful responses. Here's a step-by-step breakdown:

1. **User Query**: The user submits a query.

2. **Retrieve**: The retriever searches a knowledge base to find relevant data.
3. **Generate**: The generator combines the retrieved data and user query to produce a response.
4. **Deliver**: The system outputs the final response to the user.

This separation of duties ensures efficiency and scalability, while also improving the accuracy of the output.

Example Workflow

Let's implement a basic RAG workflow using Python. We'll set up a retriever with **FAISS** and use a pretrained generator from Hugging Face.

Step 1: Creating a FAISS Index for Retrieval

First, we'll index some data to enable efficient similarity search.

import faiss

import numpy as np

Create a dataset of 100 sample document embeddings (128-dimensional vectors)

data = np.random.random((100, 128)).astype('float32')

Initialize a FAISS index

index = faiss.IndexFlatL2(128)   # L2 distance metric

index.add(data)

```
print(f"Number of vectors in the index: {index.ntotal}")
```

Step 2: Querying the Retriever

We'll query the retriever with a sample vector to get the most relevant documents.

```
# Create a query vector (128-dimensional)
query_vector = np.random.random((1, 128)).astype('float32')


# Retrieve the top 3 most similar vectors
k = 3
distances, indices = index.search(query_vector, k)
```

```
print("Distances:", distances)

print("Indices of retrieved documents:", indices)
```

Step 3: Generating a Response

Next, we use a pretrained language model to generate a response based on the retrieved documents.

```
from transformers import GPT2LMHeadModel, GPT2Tokenizer


# Load GPT-2 model and tokenizer

model_name = "gpt2"

model = GPT2LMHeadModel.from_pretrained(model_name)
```

```python
tokenizer = GPT2Tokenizer.from_pretrained(model_name)


# Combine retrieved document IDs into a context
retrieved_docs = [f"Document {i}" for i in indices[0]]
query = "What is RAG?"
input_prompt = f"Context: {' '.join(retrieved_docs)}\n\nQuery: {query}\n\nResponse:"


# Generate a response
inputs = tokenizer(input_prompt, return_tensors="pt")
outputs = model.generate(inputs["input_ids"],
```

```
    max_length=150,
    num_return_sequences=1)

# Decode and print the generated response
response = tokenizer.decode(outputs[0], skip_special_tokens=True)
print("Generated Response:", response)
```

Exercise: Building the Pipeline

Objective: Create a functional two-stage RAG pipeline that retrieves and generates responses.

Exercise Steps:

1. **Set up a FAISS retriever** with sample data.

2. **Create a user query** and retrieve relevant information.
3. **Generate a response** using a pretrained language model.
4. **Test the pipeline** with different queries and verify the results.

Code Implementation

Step 1: FAISS Retriever

```
import faiss

import numpy as np

from transformers import GPT2LMHeadModel, GPT2Tokenizer


# Indexing data

data = np.random.random((100, 128)).astype('float32')

index = faiss.IndexFlatL2(128)

index.add(data)
```

```python
# Querying data
query_vector = np.random.random((1, 128)).astype('float32')
k = 3
distances, indices = index.search(query_vector, k)


# Step 2: Generator
retrieved_docs = [f"Document {i}" for i in indices[0]]
query = "Explain the role of retrievers in RAG."
input_prompt = f"Context: {' '.join(retrieved_docs)}\n\nQuery: {query}\n\nResponse:"
```

```python
# Load GPT-2
model_name = "gpt2"
model = GPT2LMHeadModel.from_pretrained(model_name)
tokenizer = GPT2Tokenizer.from_pretrained(model_name)


# Generate response
inputs = tokenizer(input_prompt, return_tensors="pt")
outputs = model.generate(inputs["input_ids"], max_length=150)
response = tokenizer.decode(outputs[0], skip_special_tokens=True)
```

print("Final Response:", response)

The two-stage pipeline of RAG provides a structured and scalable approach to building intelligent systems. The retriever ensures relevance, while the generator provides coherence and natural language fluency. By implementing the steps and examples outlined above, you can start building your own RAG pipeline, optimizing it for your specific use cases.

4.2 Designing the Retriever: Indexing and Querying Data

The retriever is the backbone of the Retrieval-Augmented Generation (RAG) architecture. Its main purpose is to efficiently locate and return the most relevant pieces of information from a knowledge base. This process is achieved through **indexing** and **querying**.

In this section, we'll walk through the design of a robust retriever, focusing on how to index data effectively and query it with precision. By the end of this chapter, you'll have a clear understanding of these concepts and practical skills to implement them in your own projects.

Understanding Indexing and Querying

- **Indexing**: The process of organizing data in a way that enables fast and accurate retrieval. Think of it as building a "searchable map" of your data.
- **Querying**: The act of searching the indexed data to find items relevant to a given query.

The goal of this two-step process is to balance speed and accuracy, ensuring that relevant information is retrieved quickly, even from large datasets.

Indexing Data for Efficient Retrieval

For indexing, we'll use **FAISS** (Facebook AI Similarity Search), a popular library for fast similarity searches. FAISS works by converting textual data into **dense vectors** using embeddings and then organizing these vectors for quick lookup.

Steps to Index Data

1. **Prepare Your Data**: Start with a collection of textual documents or structured data.
2. **Generate Embeddings**: Convert the data into numerical vectors using a pre-trained model like **SentenceTransformers**.

3. **Build the Index**: Use FAISS to organize these vectors for efficient similarity searches.

Practical Example: Indexing Documents

Using Python, we'll index a set of documents with FAISS:

Step 1: Install required libraries

pip install faiss-cpu sentence-transformers

import faiss

from sentence_transformers import SentenceTransformer

import numpy as np

Step 2: Prepare sample documents

documents = [

"RAG stands for Retrieval-Augmented Generation.",

"The retriever fetches relevant data from a knowledge base.",

"FAISS is a library for efficient similarity searches.",

"Transformers are widely used for generating embeddings."

]

Step 3: Generate embeddings

model = SentenceTransformer('all-MiniLM-L6-v2')   # Pre-trained embedding model

embeddings = model.encode(documents) # Convert text to vectors

```
embeddings = np.array(embeddings).astype('float32')  # Ensure correct type for FAISS


# Step 4: Create a FAISS index

dimension = embeddings.shape[1]  # Dimensionality of the embeddings

index = faiss.IndexFlatL2(dimension)  # L2 distance metric

index.add(embeddings)  # Add embeddings to the index


print(f"Number of items in the index: {index.ntotal}")
```

Querying the Indexed Data

Once the data is indexed, you can query it using a vector representation of a search term. The retriever will return the most similar entries from the index.

Steps to Query the Index

1. **Generate a Query Vector**: Use the same embedding model to convert your query into a vector.
2. **Search the Index**: Retrieve the top N most similar items using FAISS.
3. **Interpret Results**: Map the retrieved vectors back to their original documents.

Example: Querying the Index

Step 1: Create a query

query = "What is FAISS used for?"

query_vector = model.encode([query]).astype('float32') # Generate query vector

```python
# Step 2: Search the index
k = 2  # Number of results to retrieve
distances, indices = index.search(query_vector, k)


# Step 3: Map results back to documents
print("Query:", query)
print("Retrieved Documents:")
for i, idx in enumerate(indices[0]):
    print(f"{i+1}. {documents[idx]} (Score: {distances[0][i]})")
```

Output:

Query: What is FAISS used for?

Retrieved Documents:

1. FAISS is a library for efficient similarity searches. (Score: 0.84)

2. RAG stands for Retrieval-Augmented Generation. (Score: 1.12)

Real-World Applications of Indexing and Querying

1. **Chatbots**: Quickly retrieve relevant knowledge base entries to answer user queries.
2. **Search Engines**: Enable faster and more accurate document searches.
3. **Recommendation Systems**: Suggest similar products or content based on user preferences.

Exercise: Building a Complete Retriever

Objective: Create a fully functional retriever that indexes and queries a dataset of textual documents.

Steps:

1. **Prepare a dataset** of at least 50 textual entries.
2. **Generate embeddings** using a pre-trained model.
3. **Index the data** with FAISS.
4. **Create a query interface** to input a search term and retrieve results.

Code Implementation

```
# Full implementation of a retriever


# Dataset

documents = [
```

```python
    f"Document {i}: Sample text for document {i}" for i in range(50)
]

# Generate embeddings
embeddings = model.encode(documents).astype('float32')

# Create and populate FAISS index
dimension = embeddings.shape[1]
index = faiss.IndexFlatL2(dimension)
index.add(embeddings)

# Query function
def query_retriever(query, top_k=3):
```

```
    query_vector = model.encode([query]).astype('float32')

    distances, indices = index.search(query_vector, top_k)

    return [(documents[idx], distances[0][i]) for i, idx in enumerate(indices[0])]


# Example usage
results = query_retriever("Sample text for document", top_k=5)

for i, (doc, score) in enumerate(results):
    print(f"{i+1}. {doc} (Score: {score})")
```

In this chapter, you learned how to design an efficient retriever by indexing and querying data. The **indexing process** organizes data for fast searches, while the **querying process** ensures relevant information is retrieved accurately. By following the examples and exercises, you now have the tools to build a robust retriever that can serve as the backbone of your RAG workflow.

4.3 Connecting the Generator: Generating Context-Aware Responses

The generator is the heart of a RAG system, responsible for crafting meaningful and context-aware responses based on retrieved data. While the retriever fetches relevant pieces of information, the generator uses this input to produce coherent, natural language outputs.

In this section, we'll dive into the mechanics of integrating a generator into your RAG architecture. We will explore step-by-step how to use pre-trained language models such as OpenAI's GPT or Hugging Face Transformers to craft context-aware responses. Practical examples and well-commented code will guide you through this process.

The Role of the Generator in RAG

The generator bridges the gap between raw data and user-friendly responses. It processes the retrieved information, contextualizes it, and outputs a response that is:

1. **Accurate**: Reflects the essence of the retrieved data.
2. **Coherent**: Reads naturally, making sense in context.

3. **Engaging**: Presents information in a conversational manner.

Setting Up the Generator

To connect the generator, we need a pre-trained language model capable of processing input text and generating relevant responses. Here, we'll use OpenAI's GPT-3.5 or Hugging Face's models like `t5-large` or `GPT-2`.

Installation Requirements

Ensure you have the following installed:

- Python 3.7 or above
- Hugging Face Transformers (`pip install transformers`)
- OpenAI's SDK (for GPT models, `pip install openai`)

Choosing a Pre-Trained Model

- **OpenAI GPT-3.5**: Ideal for highly fluent and detailed responses. Requires an API key.
- **Hugging Face Transformers**: Open-source and versatile for many tasks, though it may require fine-tuning for best results.

Integrating the Generator

Step 1: Generate Responses Using OpenAI GPT-3.5

Here's how to connect GPT-3.5 as your generator:

Install the OpenAI library: pip install openai

import openai

```
# Set your OpenAI API key

openai.api_key = "your-openai-api-key"


# Function to generate responses

def generate_response_with_gpt(query, context):

    prompt = f"""

    You are an intelligent assistant. Use the following context to answer the user's query:


    Context: {context}

    Query: {query}


    Answer:
```

```
    """

    response = openai.Completion.create(
        engine="text-davinci-003",  # GPT-3.5 engine
        prompt=prompt,
        max_tokens=150,
        temperature=0.7
    )
    return response.choices[0].text.strip()


# Example usage
query = "What is RAG architecture?"
context = "RAG combines a retriever and generator to answer complex questions."
```

response = generate_response_with_gpt(query, context)

print("Generated Response:", response)

Step 2: Generate Responses Using Hugging Face Transformers

For an open-source alternative, use Hugging Face's T5 or GPT models:

Install required libraries: pip install transformers

from transformers import pipeline

Load a pre-trained text generation model

generator = pipeline("text2text-generation", model="t5-large")

```python
# Function to generate responses
def generate_response_with_t5(query, context):
    input_text = f"Context: {context} Query: {query}"
    response = generator(input_text, max_length=100, num_return_sequences=1)
    return response[0]['generated_text']


# Example usage
query = "What is RAG architecture?"
context = "RAG combines a retriever and generator to answer complex questions."
```

```
response = generate_response_with_t5(query, context)

print("Generated Response:", response)
```

Creating Context-Aware Responses

Context-aware responses require combining the retriever and generator. This ensures the generator uses the most relevant data when crafting its response.

Practical Example: A Unified Retriever and Generator Workflow

```
# Combining Retriever and Generator

def unified_rag_workflow(query, retriever, generator):

    # Step 1: Retrieve relevant context
```

```
context = retriever(query)

# Step 2: Generate a response using the context

response = generator(query, context)

return response


# Example usage with placeholder retriever and generator

def mock_retriever(query):

    # Simulated retrieval step

    return "RAG combines retrievers and generators for context-aware responses."
```

```
def mock_generator(query, context):

    return f"Based on the context: '{context}', the query '{query}' can be answered as follows: RAG is a hybrid architecture for enhanced AI performance."


query = "What is the role of a generator in RAG?"

response = unified_rag_workflow(query, mock_retriever, mock_generator)

print(response)
```

Optimizing Generated Responses

To ensure high-quality responses:

1. **Refine Prompts**: Tailor prompts to guide the generator effectively.
2. **Limit Token Count**: Keep outputs concise by setting a maximum token limit.
3. **Experiment with Parameters**: Adjust temperature and top-p values for variability in responses.

Real-World Applications

1. **Customer Support**: Generate accurate answers from a knowledge base.
2. **Content Creation**: Automate writing based on contextual data.
3. **Educational Tools**: Provide detailed explanations and solutions.

Hands-On Exercise: Building a Simple RAG API

Objective: Develop an API that combines retrieval and generation.

Code Implementation

```python
from flask import Flask, request, jsonify


app = Flask(__name__)


# Mock functions for retriever and generator

def retriever(query):
    return "This is a mock retrieved context relevant to the query."


def generator(query, context):
```

```
    return f"Using the context: '{context}', the answer to '{query}' is this generated response."


@app.route('/rag', methods=['POST'])
def rag_endpoint():
    data = request.json
    query = data.get("query")

    # Step 1: Retrieve context
    context = retriever(query)

    # Step 2: Generate response
    response = generator(query, context)
```

```
    return jsonify({"query": query, "context": context, "response": response})

if __name__ == "__main__":
    app.run(debug=True)
```

Test the API

Send a POST request to /rag with a query payload:
```
{
    "query": "What is RAG?"
}
```

•

In this chapter, we explored how to connect the generator in a RAG architecture, transforming retrieved information into meaningful, context-aware responses. With practical examples and a hands-on exercise, you now have the tools to integrate and optimize a generator for your own RAG workflows.

4.4 Optimizing for Scalability and Performance

As your Retrieval-Augmented Generation (RAG) system grows, ensuring it operates efficiently under increasing loads becomes critical. Scalability and performance optimization are key factors to handle large datasets, high query volumes, and complex generation tasks without compromising speed or accuracy.

This chapter focuses on best practices, tools, and techniques to make your RAG system scalable and high-performing. You'll learn how to optimize data storage, querying, and response generation, all while maintaining system reliability.

Key Goals of Optimization

1. **Scalability**: Ensure the system can handle increasing data sizes and query demands by scaling horizontally (adding more machines) or vertically (enhancing resources on existing machines).
2. **Performance**: Minimize latency and improve throughput to deliver fast and accurate responses.

Techniques for Optimization

1. Efficient Data Indexing and Retrieval

A well-optimized retriever is the foundation of a scalable RAG system.

Best Practices

- **Choose the Right Index Type**: For large-scale retrieval, use vector-based search systems like FAISS, Elasticsearch, or Pinecone.
- **Reduce Index Size**: Use dimensionality reduction techniques like PCA to compress embeddings without significant loss in accuracy.
- **Implement Caching**: Cache frequently accessed results to avoid repeated computation.

Practical Example: FAISS Index Optimization

```
import faiss
import numpy as np

# Create dummy data (100,000 vectors of size 512)
data = np.random.random((100000, 512)).astype('float32')

# Step 1: Dimensionality reduction with PCA
d = 512  # Original dimension
d_reduced = 128  # Reduced dimension

pca_matrix = faiss.PCAMatrix(d, d_reduced)
```

```python
pca_matrix.train(data)

data_reduced = pca_matrix.apply_py(data)


# Step 2: Create FAISS index

index = faiss.IndexFlatL2(d_reduced)  # L2 similarity search

index.add(data_reduced)  # Add reduced vectors to the index


# Search

query_vector = np.random.random((1, 512)).astype('float32')

query_vector_reduced = pca_matrix.apply_py(query_vector)

distances, indices = index.search(query_vector_reduced, k=5)
```

print(f"Nearest neighbors: {indices}, Distances: {distances}")

This reduces memory usage and speeds up search queries, making the retriever more efficient.

---

2. Asynchronous Operations

To handle multiple concurrent queries, implement asynchronous workflows for both the retriever and generator.

Practical Example: Asynchronous Retrieval and Generation

Using Python's `asyncio` library:

import asyncio

```python
async def retriever(query):
    await asyncio.sleep(1)  # Simulate retrieval delay
    return f"Context for query '{query}' retrieved."


async def generator(context):
    await asyncio.sleep(2)  # Simulate generation delay
    return f"Generated response using context: {context}"


async def process_query(query):
    context = await retriever(query)
    response = await generator(context)
    return response
```

```python
async def main():
    queries = ["What is RAG?", "Explain scalability in AI.", "What is FAISS?"]
    tasks = [process_query(query) for query in queries]

    results = await asyncio.gather(*tasks)
    for i, result in enumerate(results):
        print(f"Query {i+1}: {result}")

# Run the asynchronous workflow
asyncio.run(main())
```

This approach handles multiple requests in parallel, reducing overall latency.

3. Load Balancing

Distribute incoming requests across multiple servers to prevent overload.

Implementation with NGINX

1. Install and configure **NGINX** as a reverse proxy.
2. Add the following configuration to `nginx.conf`:

http {

  upstream backend_servers {

    server server1.example.com;

    server server2.example.com;

  }

  server {

    listen 80;

    location / {

```
        proxy_pass
http://backend_servers;

    }
  }
}
```

This ensures that queries are distributed evenly across backend servers.

---

4. Optimizing the Generator

Fine-Tune Models

Instead of relying on large pre-trained models, fine-tune smaller models on your specific dataset to improve response speed and accuracy.

Batch Processing for Generations

Process multiple queries simultaneously for better resource utilization.

from transformers import pipeline

Load a text generation pipeline

```
generator = pipeline("text-generation", model="gpt2")
```

Batch processing

```
queries = [
    "What is RAG?",
    "Explain vector search.",
    "What is dimensionality reduction?"
]
contexts = [
```

"RAG is a hybrid architecture combining retrieval and generation.",

"Vector search uses embeddings for information retrieval.",

"Dimensionality reduction reduces the size of feature vectors."

]


```
batch_input = [f"Context: {c} Query: {q}" for c, q in zip(contexts, queries)]

responses = generator(batch_input, max_length=100, num_return_sequences=1)


for i, response in enumerate(responses):
    print(f"Query {i+1}: {response['generated_text']}")
```

5. Monitoring and Debugging

Track system performance with tools like **Prometheus** and **Grafana** for real-time metrics.

Example: Monitoring Latency

1. Install **Prometheus** and **Grafana**.
2. Configure Prometheus to scrape application metrics.
3. Instrument your Python application with `prometheus_client`:

```
from prometheus_client import start_http_server, Summary
import time


# Create a metric to track query latency
```

```python
REQUEST_TIME = Summary('request_processing_seconds', 'Time spent processing a request')

@REQUEST_TIME.time()
def process_query(query):
    time.sleep(2)  # Simulate processing
    return f"Response for query '{query}'"

if __name__ == "__main__":
    start_http_server(8000)  # Expose metrics on port 8000
    while True:
        process_query("Sample Query")
```

Access metrics at `http://localhost:8000/metrics` and visualize them in Grafana.

Scaling RAG in the Cloud

To scale your RAG system globally, deploy it on cloud platforms like AWS, Azure, or GCP.

Key Features to Leverage

- **Auto-scaling Groups**: Automatically adjust resources based on demand.
- **Serverless Functions**: For lightweight, on-demand processing (e.g., AWS Lambda).
- **Content Delivery Networks (CDNs)**: Cache responses close to users for faster access.

Real-World Use Case: A Scalable RAG System for Customer Support

A tech company deploys a RAG-based chatbot to handle support queries. By combining the above techniques:

1. **Efficient Indexing**: FAISS reduces query time for their large knowledge base.
2. **Asynchronous Workflow**: Handles thousands of simultaneous queries.
3. **Load Balancing**: Distributes traffic across multiple cloud servers.
4. **Batch Generation**: Answers grouped queries efficiently.

Result: The system supports millions of daily users with minimal latency and high reliability.

Hands-On Exercise: Build and Benchmark Your RAG System

Objective: Develop a RAG system and benchmark its scalability.

1. Implement retrieval and generation workflows from previous chapters.
2. Deploy the system with a load balancer (e.g., NGINX).
3. Use **Apache JMeter** to simulate concurrent users and measure system performance.

Optimizing for scalability and performance ensures your RAG system remains responsive and efficient as demands grow. By implementing strategies like efficient indexing, asynchronous operations, load balancing, and cloud scaling, you can build a robust system ready for real-world applications. Use these techniques to elevate your RAG architecture to production-level performance.

Chapter 5. Practical Hands-On Projects

5.1 FAQ Retrieval System

Building an FAQ retrieval system with RAG provides a practical example of how you can combine structured data with the power of LLMs. This project walks you through the steps to create a knowledge base, implement a retrieval mechanism with dense vector search, and enhance responses with LLMs.

Step 1: Creating a Knowledge Base from Scratch

To start, let's build a structured knowledge base that will serve as the backbone for our FAQ system.

```python
import pandas as pd

# Step 1: Define FAQ questions and answers
faq_data = {
    "question": [
        "What is RAG?",
        "How does dense vector search work?",
        "What are LLMs used for in RAG?",
        "How can I integrate RAG into my application?"
    ],
    "answer": [
        "RAG, or Retrieval-Augmented Generation, is a system that combines information retrieval and language
```

models to generate context-aware responses.",

"Dense vector search finds similar data points by comparing vector representations of queries and documents.",

"LLMs in RAG generate detailed and context-aware answers using retrieved data.",

"You can integrate RAG by combining a retriever, such as FAISS, with an LLM like OpenAI's GPT."

    ]

}

Step 2: Convert the data to a pandas DataFrame

faq_df = pd.DataFrame(faq_data)

```
# Step 3: Save the knowledge base to a CSV file
faq_df.to_csv("faq_knowledge_base.csv", index=False)

print("Knowledge base created and saved as 'faq_knowledge_base.csv'")
```

This code creates a knowledge base and stores it in a CSV file. The CSV format ensures that the data can be easily loaded and updated as needed.

Step 2: Implementing Retrieval with Dense Vector Search

Dense vector search improves the accuracy of information retrieval by leveraging embeddings generated from a language model. Here's how to implement it:

```python
from sentence_transformers import SentenceTransformer
import faiss
import pandas as pd


# Step 1: Load the knowledge base
faq_df = pd.read_csv("faq_knowledge_base.csv")
questions = faq_df["question"].tolist()


# Step 2: Generate vector embeddings for the questions
model = SentenceTransformer('all-MiniLM-L6-v2')  # Pre-trained embedding model
```

```python
question_embeddings = model.encode(questions, convert_to_numpy=True)


# Step 3: Create a FAISS index for efficient search
dimension = question_embeddings.shape[1]
index = faiss.IndexFlatL2(dimension)
index.add(question_embeddings)


# Step 4: Query the index
query = "How does RAG work?"
query_embedding = model.encode([query], convert_to_numpy=True)
```

```python
# Step 5: Search for the closest match
distances, indices = index.search(query_embedding, k=1)

# Retrieve the closest match
retrieved_question = questions[indices[0][0]]
retrieved_answer = faq_df["answer"].iloc[indices[0][0]]

print(f"Query: {query}")
print(f"Matched Question: {retrieved_question}")
print(f"Answer: {retrieved_answer}")
```

This implementation ensures fast and accurate retrieval of FAQs, even as the dataset grows.

Step 3: Generating Contextual Answers with LLMs

Once the most relevant FAQ is retrieved, you can use an LLM to generate a more detailed and context-aware response.

from transformers import pipeline

Step 1: Load a pre-trained LLM for text generation

generator = pipeline("text-generation", model="gpt2")

```python
# Step 2: Combine the retrieved answer with the query for context-aware generation
input_text = f"User Query: {query}\nRetrieved Answer: {retrieved_answer}\nGenerate a detailed response:"

# Step 3: Generate a response
response = generator(input_text, max_length=100, num_return_sequences=1)

print(f"Generated Response: {response[0]['generated_text']}")
```

By combining retrieval with generation, you create a system that provides detailed and nuanced answers while keeping computation efficient.

Practical Exercises

1. **Expand the Knowledge Base**

    - Add more entries to the knowledge base, covering topics relevant to your application domain.
    - Test retrieval accuracy for various user queries.

2. **Experiment with Retrieval Models**

    - Replace the `all-MiniLM-L6-v2` model with other sentence embedding models like `sentence-transformers/multi-qa-MiniLM-L6-cos-v1` and observe performance differences.

3. **Optimize LLM Generation**

    o Try different pre-trained LLMs, such as OpenAI's GPT or Hugging Face models, to evaluate which produces the most accurate responses.

Example

If you're creating an FAQ bot for a tech support company. Your knowledge base might include common troubleshooting steps, product details, and contact information. A query like *"How can I update my account password?"* would retrieve the closest FAQ: *"To reset your password, go to settings and click on 'Forgot Password'."* The LLM could then generate a detailed explanation, including additional security tips.

This hands-on project demonstrated how to build an FAQ retrieval system using RAG principles. By creating a structured knowledge base, implementing dense vector search, and leveraging LLMs, you can deliver highly relevant and contextual answers to user queries. These skills form the foundation for more advanced applications like conversational agents and domain-specific information retrieval systems.

5.2 Conversational AI with RAG

Building a chatbot that can efficiently handle domain-specific queries and maintain context over multiple turns is one of the most impactful applications of Retrieval-Augmented Generation (RAG). In this section, we'll guide you through creating a conversational AI system that uses RAG to provide accurate, context-aware responses tailored to specific use cases.

Building a Chatbot for Domain-Specific Use Cases

A chatbot with domain-specific knowledge requires a structured knowledge base, a retriever for fetching relevant data, and a generator for crafting human-like responses.

Step 1: Preparing the Knowledge Base

Start with a domain-specific knowledge base. For instance, let's build a dataset for an e-commerce chatbot.

import pandas as pd

Create a knowledge base for an e-commerce domain

```
data = {
    "question": [
        "What are the return policies?",
        "How can I track my order?",
        "Do you offer discounts on bulk purchases?",
        "What payment methods do you accept?"
    ],
    "answer": [
        "Our return policy allows returns within 30 days of purchase. Items must be unused and in original packaging.",
        "You can track your order by logging into your account and clicking on 'Track Order' in the dashboard.",
```

"Yes, we offer discounts for bulk purchases. Please contact our sales team for more details.",

"We accept credit cards, debit cards, PayPal, and bank transfers."

   ]
}


```
# Save the knowledge base
knowledge_base = pd.DataFrame(data)
knowledge_base.to_csv("ecommerce_knowledge_base.csv", index=False)
print("Knowledge base created and saved.")
```

This knowledge base contains domain-specific FAQs, which the chatbot will use to generate responses.

Step 2: Implementing the Retriever

A retriever finds the most relevant entry in the knowledge base for a user query. We'll use **Sentence Transformers** for embedding and **FAISS** for retrieval.

```
from sentence_transformers import SentenceTransformer
import faiss


# Load the knowledge base
knowledge_base = pd.read_csv("ecommerce_knowledge_base.csv")
questions = knowledge_base["question"].tolist()


# Generate embeddings for questions
```

```python
embedder = SentenceTransformer("all-MiniLM-L6-v2")

question_embeddings = embedder.encode(questions, convert_to_numpy=True)


# Create a FAISS index for efficient retrieval
dimension = question_embeddings.shape[1]
index = faiss.IndexFlatL2(dimension)
index.add(question_embeddings)


def retrieve(query):
    """Retrieve the most relevant answer for a given query."""
```

```python
    query_embedding = embedder.encode([query], convert_to_numpy=True)

    distances, indices = index.search(query_embedding, k=1)

    best_match = indices[0][0]

    return knowledge_base.iloc[best_match]["answer"]


# Test retrieval
query = "How do I return an item?"

retrieved_answer = retrieve(query)

print(f"Query: {query}\nRetrieved Answer: {retrieved_answer}")
```

This retriever is designed to provide accurate responses by matching the user query to the closest entry in the knowledge base.

Step 3: Integrating the Generator

The generator refines the retrieved answer, ensuring the response is context-aware and conversational.

```
from transformers import pipeline


# Load a language generation model

generator = pipeline("text-generation", model="gpt2")


def generate_response(user_query):

    """Combine retrieval and generation for a natural language response."""
```

```python
    retrieved_answer = retrieve(user_query)

    input_text = f"User Query: {user_query}\nAnswer: {retrieved_answer}\nRespond conversationally:"

    response = generator(input_text, max_length=100, num_return_sequences=1)

    return response[0]["generated_text"]


# Test the generator

user_query = "Do you provide bulk discounts?"

response = generate_response(user_query)

print(f"Chatbot Response: {response}")
```

The generator ensures that the chatbot responses sound natural and engaging.

Handling Multi-Turn Conversations Using RAG

Multi-turn conversations require tracking the dialogue context to provide meaningful responses that build upon previous exchanges.

Step 1: Implementing a Context Manager

A context manager keeps track of the conversation's flow.

```
class ContextManager:
    def __init__(self):
        self.context = []
```

```python
def add_to_context(self, user_query, bot_response):
    """Add the latest interaction to the context."""
    self.context.append({"user": user_query, "bot": bot_response})
    if len(self.context) > 5:  # Limit to the last 5 interactions
        self.context.pop(0)


def get_context(self):
    """Retrieve the full conversation context."""
    return "\n".join(
        [f"User: {turn['user']}\nBot: {turn['bot']}" for turn in self.context]
    )
```

Example usage

context_manager = ContextManager()

context_manager.add_to_context("What are the return policies?", "Our return policy allows returns within 30 days of purchase.")

context_manager.add_to_context("Do you provide free return shipping?", "Free return shipping is available for items above $50.")

print(context_manager.get_context())

Step 2: Combining Retrieval, Generation, and Context

We'll integrate the context manager with the retriever and generator to handle ongoing conversations.

```python
def generate_contextual_response(user_query, context_manager):
    """Generate a response considering the conversation context."""
    context = context_manager.get_context()
    retrieved_answer = retrieve(user_query)
    input_text = f"Conversation Context:\n{context}\nUser Query: {user_query}\nAnswer: {retrieved_answer}\nGenerate a relevant response:"
    response = generator(input_text, max_length=150, num_return_sequences=1)
    return response[0]["generated_text"]
```

```python
# Example multi-turn conversation

context_manager = ContextManager()


# Turn 1

user_query = "What are the return policies?"

response = generate_response(user_query)

context_manager.add_to_context(user_query, response)


# Turn 2

user_query = "Do you provide free return shipping?"

response = generate_contextual_response(user_query, context_manager)
```

```
context_manager.add_to_context(user
_query, response)
```

```
print(f"Chatbot Response:\n{response}")
```

Practical Exercises

1. **Customize the Knowledge Base**
   Create a knowledge base for a different domain, such as healthcare or education. Test how well your chatbot adapts.

2. **Enhance Context Management**
   Implement a more advanced context manager using token limits or conversation segmentation.

3. **Experiment with Generators**
   Try different LLMs (e.g., OpenAI's

GPT-4 or Hugging Face's Falcon) and compare response quality.

Real-World Application

This system can be used to build domain-specific virtual assistants, such as:

- A customer service bot for e-commerce platforms.
- A help desk assistant for IT queries.
- A medical advisor for basic healthcare FAQs.

5.3 RAG for Summarizing Large Datasets

In the era of information overload, summarizing large datasets is a crucial task for extracting key insights efficiently. Retrieval-Augmented

Generation (RAG) combines the power of data retrieval and generative AI to create concise, relevant summaries of vast textual databases. This chapter walks you through building a RAG-based summarization system, from indexing data to generating high-quality summaries.

Indexing Large Textual Databases

The first step in summarizing datasets is to structure the data for efficient retrieval. We will index the data using dense vector representations, which allow us to find relevant sections of text based on semantic similarity.

Step 1: Preparing the Dataset

Let's use an example dataset containing research articles.

import pandas as pd

```python
# Sample dataset of research articles
data = {
    "id": [1, 2, 3],
    "title": [
        "The Impact of Climate Change on Marine Ecosystems",
        "Advances in Quantum Computing Algorithms",
        "Understanding the Human Genome Project"
    ],
    "content": [
        "Climate change affects marine biodiversity by altering temperature, oxygen levels, and ocean acidity.",
```

"Quantum computing promises faster solutions to complex problems like cryptography and molecular simulations.",

"The Human Genome Project has revolutionized biology, providing insights into genetic diseases and evolution."

]

}

Create a DataFrame and save it

df = pd.DataFrame(data)

df.to_csv("research_articles.csv", index=False)

print("Dataset prepared and saved.")

This dataset simulates a collection of documents, each with an ID, title, and content.

Step 2: Embedding and Indexing

Use **Sentence Transformers** for embeddings and **FAISS** for creating a vector index.

from sentence_transformers import SentenceTransformer

import faiss

import numpy as np

Load the dataset

df = pd.read_csv("research_articles.csv")

contents = df["content"].tolist()

```python
# Generate embeddings
embedder = SentenceTransformer("all-MiniLM-L6-v2")
embeddings = embedder.encode(contents, convert_to_numpy=True)


# Create a FAISS index
dimension = embeddings.shape[1]
index = faiss.IndexFlatL2(dimension)
index.add(embeddings)


# Save the index for reuse
faiss.write_index(index, "content_index.faiss")
```

print("Index created and saved.")

This code creates a searchable vector index of the dataset's content, enabling fast and accurate retrieval.

Generating Concise and Relevant Summaries

After retrieving relevant sections of the dataset, the next step is to generate summaries. This involves fine-tuning an LLM to process and condense the retrieved text.

Step 1: Retrieving Relevant Data

Let's retrieve text based on a user query.

```
def retrieve_text(query, top_k=1):

    """Retrieve the most relevant sections of text."""
```

```python
    query_embedding = embedder.encode([query], convert_to_numpy=True)

    distances, indices = index.search(query_embedding, k=top_k)

    retrieved_texts = [contents[i] for i in indices[0]]

    return retrieved_texts


# Test retrieval
query = "How does climate change affect marine life?"

retrieved = retrieve_text(query)

print(f"Query: {query}\nRetrieved: {retrieved}")
```

This function retrieves sections of the dataset most relevant to the query.

Step 2: Summarizing Retrieved Data

Use a summarization model, such as **Hugging Face's T5**, to create concise summaries.

```
from transformers import pipeline

# Load a summarization model
summarizer = pipeline("summarization", model="t5-small")

def summarize_text(text):
    """Generate a summary for a given text."""
```

```
    summary = summarizer(text,
max_length=50, min_length=10,
do_sample=False)

    return summary[0]["summary_text"]


# Test summarization

text_to_summarize = retrieved[0]

summary = summarize_text(text_to_summarize)

print(f"Original Text: {text_to_summarize}\nSummary: {summary}")
```

This model produces a concise summary of the retrieved text while maintaining its key information.

Step 3: Combining Retrieval and Summarization

We'll now combine retrieval and summarization into a single workflow.

```
def generate_summary(query):
    """Retrieve relevant text and generate a summary."""
    retrieved_texts = retrieve_text(query, top_k=2)
    combined_text = " ".join(retrieved_texts)
    summary = summarize_text(combined_text)
    return summary

# Test the system
```

```
query = "Discuss advancements in quantum computing."

summary = generate_summary(query)

print(f"Query: {query}\nSummary: {summary}")
```

This end-to-end function retrieves the most relevant data and generates a meaningful summary.

Practical Exercises

1. **Experiment with Dataset Sizes**
   Try scaling the dataset to include hundreds or thousands of entries. Measure retrieval speed and accuracy.

2. **Fine-Tune the Summarizer**
   Use domain-specific data to fine-

tune a summarization model for better results in specialized fields.

3. **Integrate Contextual Queries**
   Enhance the retrieval function to consider query context for more precise results.

Real-World Application

RAG-based summarization can be applied to:

- **Scientific Research**: Summarizing papers for researchers.
- **Legal Documents**: Extracting key clauses from contracts.
- **Customer Support**: Summarizing ticket histories for quicker resolution.

In this chapter, we explored how to build a system that uses RAG to summarize large datasets. By indexing data with vector embeddings and leveraging summarization models, we created a powerful tool for condensing vast amounts of text into actionable insights. With a structured approach and hands-on examples, you now have the tools to tackle large-scale summarization challenges effectively.

Chapter 6. Advanced Techniques and Optimizations

In this chapter, we'll explore cutting-edge techniques to enhance the performance, accuracy, and scalability of Retrieval-Augmented Generation (RAG) systems. By delving into dense embeddings, fine-tuning generative models, and optimizing for enterprise and real-time use cases, we'll equip you with the tools to elevate your RAG implementations to a professional level.

6.1 Enhancing Retrieval Accuracy with Dense Embeddings

Dense embeddings have transformed information retrieval by providing a way to represent textual data in high-dimensional vectors, capturing semantic meaning rather than relying solely on surface-level keywords. This allows systems to retrieve content that is more contextually relevant, leading to significant improvements in user experience.

In this section, we will explore how to enhance retrieval accuracy with dense embeddings. We'll start by understanding their role, move on to practical implementation using state-of-the-art libraries, and conclude with optimization techniques for better performance.

What Are Dense Embeddings?

Dense embeddings are numerical representations of text, designed to capture semantic relationships. Unlike traditional methods like TF-IDF, which rely on word frequency, dense embeddings encode the context and meaning of words in a high-dimensional vector space.

For instance:

- The sentence "Machine learning algorithms are powerful" might have a similar embedding to "AI models are highly effective" because of their semantic similarity.

Step 1: Setting Up a Dense Embedding Model

Libraries like **Sentence Transformers** make it easy to generate dense embeddings. Let's start by loading a pre-trained embedding model and generating vectors for sample text data.

Code Example: Generating Dense Embeddings

Install the required library if not already installed

!pip install sentence-transformers

from sentence_transformers import SentenceTransformer

Load a pre-trained dense embedding model

model = SentenceTransformer("all-MiniLM-L6-v2") # Lightweight, high-performance model

Sample documents for retrieval

documents = [

"Deep learning techniques are widely used in natural language processing.",

"Climate change affects ecosystems around the world.",

"Quantum computing is revolutionizing encryption and problem-solving."
]

Generate dense embeddings for the documents

embeddings = model.encode(documents, convert_to_numpy=True)

print("Embedding shape:", embeddings.shape) # Example: (3, 384)

Step 2: Retrieving Information Using Dense Embeddings

Once you have the embeddings for your documents, the next step is to retrieve relevant information based on a query. This involves calculating the similarity between the query and the document embeddings.

Code Example: Implementing Retrieval

from sklearn.metrics.pairwise import cosine_similarity

Define a user query

query = "How does climate change impact nature?"

Generate the embedding for the query

```python
query_embedding = model.encode([query], convert_to_numpy=True)

# Calculate cosine similarity between the query and document embeddings
similarities = cosine_similarity(query_embedding, embeddings)

# Find the most relevant document
most_relevant_idx = similarities[0].argmax()
print("Most relevant document:", documents[most_relevant_idx])

# Output:
```

"Climate change affects ecosystems around the world."

Step 3: Fine-Tuning Retrieval for Domain-Specific Applications

For specific use cases (e.g., legal, medical, or technical domains), fine-tuning embedding models on domain-specific data can significantly improve retrieval accuracy.

Steps for Fine-Tuning

1. Collect a dataset of domain-specific text.
2. Fine-tune a pre-trained model like **BERT** using a library such as Hugging Face Transformers.
3. Evaluate the model's performance on your specific retrieval task.

Optimization Techniques

1. Normalizing Embeddings

Normalization ensures that embeddings are unit vectors, which improves cosine similarity calculations.

import numpy as np

Normalize embeddings

normalized_embeddings = embeddings / np.linalg.norm(embeddings, axis=1, keepdims=True)

query_embedding_normalized = query_embedding / np.linalg.norm(query_embedding)

Recalculate similarity

similarities_normalized = cosine_similarity(query_embedding_normalized, normalized_embeddings)

2. Using Efficient Indexing with FAISS

For larger datasets, tools like **FAISS** (Facebook AI Similarity Search) enable faster similarity search.

import faiss

Create a FAISS index for fast similarity search

dimension = embeddings.shape[1]

index = faiss.IndexFlatL2(dimension)

Add embeddings to the index

index.add(embeddings)

```
# Perform a search

k = 1  # Number of top matches to retrieve

_, top_indices = index.search(query_embedding, k)

print("Top match:", documents[top_indices[0][0]])
```

Practical Exercise

1. **Experiment with Different Models**

    - Try other models from the Sentence Transformers library (e.g., `msmarco-distilbert-base-v3`) and observe how they impact retrieval accuracy.

2. **Fine-Tune for Your Dataset**

    o If you have a custom dataset, fine-tune a model like BERT to improve retrieval for your specific domain.

3. **Evaluate Performance**

    o Compare the retrieval accuracy of normalized embeddings vs. unnormalized embeddings.

Real-World Use Case

Building a FAQ System

Suppose you're creating an FAQ system for a company's website.

1. Generate embeddings for all FAQ entries.

2. Allow users to input queries, calculate similarities, and display the most relevant answer.

This approach improves user experience by providing precise answers rather than keyword-based matches.

Code Example: FAQ System

faq_entries = [

"What are your business hours?",

"How do I reset my password?",

"Where are your stores located?"

]

Generate embeddings for the FAQ entries

faq_embeddings = model.encode(faq_entries, convert_to_numpy=True)

```python
# User query
user_query = "Can I reset my account password?"


# Generate embedding for the query
user_query_embedding = model.encode([user_query], convert_to_numpy=True)


# Find the closest match
faq_similarities = cosine_similarity(user_query_embedding, faq_embeddings)
most_relevant_faq_idx = faq_similarities[0].argmax()
```

```
print("FAQ                    Match:",
faq_entries[most_relevant_faq_idx])
```

6.2 Fine-Tuning Generative Models for Domain-Specific Knowledge

Generative models like GPT (Generative Pre-trained Transformer) and BERT-based variants have revolutionized text generation by producing coherent, contextually accurate responses. However, out-of-the-box performance may not meet specific needs in specialized domains such as legal, medical, or technical fields. Fine-tuning these models on domain-specific data helps align their output to the context and nuances of your application.

Why Fine-Tune a Generative Model?

Pre-trained models are trained on diverse datasets, making them versatile but not precise for specialized domains. Fine-tuning involves adapting the model by training it on domain-relevant datasets. This enhances:

1. **Accuracy:** Producing outputs with domain-specific terminology.
2. **Relevance:** Tailoring responses to fit specific user requirements.
3. **Consistency:** Avoiding generic or incorrect responses in sensitive contexts.

Step 1: Preparing Your Dataset

The first step in fine-tuning is creating or obtaining a high-quality dataset for your domain. The dataset should:

- Be **clean and consistent.**
- Contain a mix of input prompts and expected outputs for your use case.
- Represent the domain comprehensively.

For instance, if fine-tuning for a medical chatbot, your dataset might include:

- Questions like: "What are the symptoms of diabetes?"
- Expected responses like: "Common symptoms of diabetes include increased thirst, frequent urination, and fatigue."

Example: Dataset Format

A typical dataset for fine-tuning GPT models may use the JSONL format:

{"prompt": "What are the symptoms of diabetes?", "completion": "The symptoms of diabetes include increased thirst, frequent urination, and fatigue."}

{"prompt": "Explain the causes of high blood pressure.", "completion": "High blood pressure is often caused by lifestyle factors such as poor diet, lack of exercise, or genetic predisposition."}

Step 2: Fine-Tuning Using OpenAI GPT Models

OpenAI provides tools for fine-tuning their models using custom datasets. Below are the steps to fine-tune a GPT model.

Requirements

Install OpenAI CLI:

pip install openai

1. Prepare your dataset and convert it into JSONL format.

Steps to Fine-Tune

Upload the Dataset Use the OpenAI CLI to validate and upload your dataset:

openai tools fine_tunes.prepare_data -f your_dataset.jsonl

1.

Initiate Fine-Tuning Start the fine-tuning process:

openai api fine_tunes.create -t "your_dataset_prepared.jsonl" -m "curie"

2. Replace `curie` with the model of your choice (e.g., `davinci` for more advanced capabilities).

3. **Monitor Progress** OpenAI provides updates during the process. Once

completed, your fine-tuned model will be available with a unique identifier.

Using the Fine-Tuned Model

Once fine-tuning is complete, you can use your custom model to generate domain-specific responses:

import openai

openai.api_key = "your-api-key"

Generate a domain-specific response

response = openai.Completion.create(

   model="your-fine-tuned-model-id",

  prompt="Explain the causes of high blood pressure.",

```
    max_tokens=100
)

print(response['choices'][0]['text'].strip())
```

Step 3: Fine-Tuning with Hugging Face Transformers

For open-source alternatives, Hugging Face's `transformers` library is a powerful tool. It allows you to fine-tune models like GPT-2 or T5 on domain-specific datasets.

Code Example: Fine-Tuning GPT-2

```
from transformers import GPT2Tokenizer, GPT2LMHeadModel

from transformers import Trainer, TrainingArguments
```

```python
from datasets import load_dataset

# Load pre-trained GPT-2 and tokenizer
model_name = "gpt2"
tokenizer = GPT2Tokenizer.from_pretrained(model_name)
model = GPT2LMHeadModel.from_pretrained(model_name)

# Load your dataset
dataset = load_dataset("json", data_files={"train": "your_dataset.jsonl"})

# Tokenize the dataset
def tokenize_function(examples):
```

```python
    return tokenizer(examples["prompt"], truncation=True, padding="max_length", max_length=128)

tokenized_datasets = dataset.map(tokenize_function, batched=True)

# Define training arguments
training_args = TrainingArguments(
    output_dir="./results",
    evaluation_strategy="epoch",
    learning_rate=5e-5,
    per_device_train_batch_size=4,
    num_train_epochs=3,
    save_steps=500,
)
```

```python
# Train the model
trainer = Trainer(
    model=model,
    args=training_args,
    train_dataset=tokenized_datasets["train"],
)

trainer.train()

# Save the fine-tuned model
model.save_pretrained("./fine_tuned_model")
tokenizer.save_pretrained("./fine_tuned_model")
```

Optimization Tips for Fine-Tuning

1. **Choose the Right Model:** Select a model size that balances performance and computational cost. For lightweight applications, smaller models like GPT-2 are sufficient, while larger models like GPT-3 or LLaMA offer better quality.

2. **Evaluate and Iterate:** Use a validation dataset to monitor performance during training. Fine-tune iteratively to prevent overfitting.

3. **Adjust Hyperparameters:** Experiment with learning rates, batch sizes, and epochs to achieve

optimal results.

Practical Exercise

1. **Prepare a Dataset:** Collect at least 100 domain-specific question-answer pairs.

2. **Fine-Tune a Small Model:** Use the Hugging Face example above to fine-tune GPT-2 on your dataset.

3. **Evaluate Performance:** Generate responses for new questions and compare their relevance and accuracy with the pre-trained model.

Real-World Use Case

Custom Medical Assistant

A hospital may require a chatbot to assist patients by answering medical queries. Fine-tuning GPT-3 on a dataset of medical questions ensures accurate and reliable responses.

- **Dataset:** Compile common patient questions and answers vetted by medical professionals.
- **Deployment:** Integrate the fine-tuned model with a web interface for patient interaction.

Example Interaction

User: What are the symptoms of flu?

Bot: Common symptoms of the flu include fever, chills, body aches, fatigue, and a cough.

6.3 Scaling RAG Systems for Enterprise Applications

Retrieval-Augmented Generation (RAG) systems are immensely powerful, but when it comes to deploying them at an enterprise level, scalability is critical. Enterprises often need to handle massive datasets, high volumes of user queries, and maintain low latency, all while ensuring data security and cost efficiency. In this chapter, we'll dive into the strategies and tools required to scale RAG systems effectively for enterprise applications.

Key Challenges in Scaling RAG Systems

1. **Data Volume:** Enterprises work with large and complex datasets that need efficient indexing and retrieval mechanisms.

2. **Query Latency:** Low response times are critical for applications like customer service or decision support.
3. **Concurrency:** Systems must handle thousands of simultaneous users without degrading performance.
4. **Cost Management:** Scaling infrastructure while keeping operational costs manageable is essential.
5. **Security and Privacy:** Enterprise systems often require compliance with regulations such as GDPR or HIPAA.

Core Strategies for Scaling RAG Systems

1. Efficient Data Indexing and Retrieval

Scaling a RAG system begins with an optimized retrieval layer. The retrieval engine must handle high query volumes while maintaining precision and recall.

- **Dense Vector Indexing:** Use dense embeddings to represent documents and queries in a high-dimensional space for semantic similarity.
- **Sharding and Replication:** Partition your data across multiple servers (sharding) and replicate indexes to ensure availability and scalability.

Example: Using FAISS for Scalable Retrieval

Facebook AI Similarity Search (FAISS) is a powerful library for dense vector search. Below is an example of indexing and searching a large dataset:

import faiss

import numpy as np

```python
# Simulated dataset of 1 million 512-dimensional vectors
num_vectors = 1_000_000
dimension = 512
data = np.random.random((num_vectors, dimension)).astype('float32')


# Create and train the FAISS index
index = faiss.IndexFlatL2(dimension)
index.add(data)


# Query the index
query_vector = np.random.random((1, dimension)).astype('float32')
distances, indices = index.search(query_vector, k=5)
```

print(f"Top 5 results indices: {indices}")

print(f"Top 5 distances: {distances}")

Scalability Tip: For massive datasets, use `faiss.IndexIVFFlat` to enable clustering for faster searches.

---

2. Scaling the Generative Component

The generation layer (e.g., an LLM) can be computationally expensive. Optimizing its usage is essential for enterprise scalability.

- **Model Quantization:** Reduce the model size by converting weights to lower precision (e.g., FP16 or INT8) without significant performance loss.

- **Batching:** Process multiple queries simultaneously to maximize hardware utilization.
- **Cache Results:** Cache common or predictable query responses to reduce unnecessary inference.

Example: Batched Inference with Hugging Face Transformers

```
from transformers import AutoTokenizer, AutoModelForSeq2SeqLM
```

```
# Load a pre-trained model
```

```
model_name = "facebook/bart-large"
```

```
tokenizer = AutoTokenizer.from_pretrained(model_name)
```

```
model = AutoModelForSeq2SeqLM.from_pretrained(model_name)
```

```python
# Batch of input queries
inputs = ["What is RAG?", "Explain vector search."]

tokenized_inputs = tokenizer(inputs, return_tensors="pt", padding=True, truncation=True)


# Generate responses in a batch
outputs = model.generate(**tokenized_inputs)

responses = [tokenizer.decode(output, skip_special_tokens=True) for output in outputs]


print(responses)
```

3. Horizontal and Vertical Scaling

- **Horizontal Scaling:** Distribute components (retrieval, generation) across multiple servers or containers. Tools like Kubernetes can automate the orchestration.
- **Vertical Scaling:** Upgrade individual servers with more memory, faster CPUs, or GPUs for higher performance.

Best Practices for Enterprise RAG Deployment

1. **Use Microservices Architecture:**

    o Split the RAG system into independent services: retrieval, generation, and user interface.

- Deploy each component separately, enabling independent scaling.
2. **Monitor and Optimize Performance:**
    - Implement monitoring tools like Prometheus and Grafana to track latency, throughput, and resource usage.
    - Profile the system regularly to identify bottlenecks.
3. **Data Pipeline Optimization:**
    - Use tools like Apache Kafka to handle real-time data ingestion and processing.
    - Automate periodic index updates to keep retrieval results relevant.

Practical Exercise: Deploying a Scalable RAG System

Objective:

Deploy a scalable RAG system for an enterprise knowledge base.

Steps:

1. **Dataset Preparation:** Collect a large dataset (e.g., company FAQs or documentation) and preprocess it using an embedding model like Sentence Transformers.

2. **Indexing:** Use FAISS for indexing. Implement sharding if your dataset exceeds the memory of a single machine.

3. **Backend Architecture:**

    - Retrieval Service: Set up an API to handle vector search queries.

- Generation Service: Deploy a model API for generating responses.
- Use a load balancer to distribute requests across multiple instances.

4. **Testing and Scaling:** Simulate concurrent users using tools like Apache JMeter or Locust. Adjust resources and configurations based on test results.

Real-World Example: Scaling for Customer Support

Scenario:

A large e-commerce platform deploys a RAG-based chatbot for customer support. The system needs to:

- Handle 10,000 concurrent queries.

- Retrieve information from a dataset containing millions of records.
- Provide responses in under 2 seconds.

Solution:

- **Retrieval:** Index product and policy documents with FAISS and shard the index across 10 servers.
- **Generation:** Use a fine-tuned GPT model hosted on GPU-enabled instances. Implement batching to process up to 32 queries simultaneously.
- **Caching:** Cache frequent queries (e.g., "How to return a product?") to serve responses in milliseconds.

Outcome: The system delivers accurate, real-time responses, improving customer satisfaction and reducing the workload on human agents.

6.4 Reducing Latency for Real-Time Applications

In real-time applications, every millisecond matters. Whether you're building a conversational chatbot, a recommendation system, or a dynamic content generator, reducing latency is crucial for maintaining seamless user experiences. In this chapter, we'll explore practical strategies to minimize latency in Retrieval-Augmented Generation (RAG) systems, ensuring they can deliver results quickly and efficiently.

Understanding Latency in RAG Systems

Latency in RAG systems primarily arises from two components:

1. **Retrieval Latency:** The time taken to fetch relevant documents or data from the retrieval engine.

2. **Generation Latency:** The time the language model requires to process input and produce a response.

By addressing bottlenecks in both areas, we can create systems capable of handling real-time requirements.

Strategies for Reducing Retrieval Latency

1. Optimizing the Retrieval Engine

Use Approximate Nearest Neighbor (ANN) Search

Instead of exact searches, ANN algorithms approximate results with significantly reduced query times. Libraries like **FAISS** and **ScaNN** are optimized for this.

Example: Fast Retrieval with FAISS

python

```python
import faiss
import numpy as np

# Simulate a large dataset of 1M vectors
dimension = 512
num_vectors = 1_000_000
data = np.random.random((num_vectors, dimension)).astype('float32')

# Create an index for approximate search
index = faiss.IndexFlatL2(dimension)  # L2 = Euclidean distance
```

```
index = faiss.IndexIVFFlat(index, dimension, nlist=100)  # IVF for clustering


# Train and add vectors to the index
index.train(data)
index.add(data)


# Search for the nearest neighbors
query_vector = np.random.random((1, dimension)).astype('float32')
index.nprobe = 10  # Search only in 10 clusters for faster queries
```

```
distances, indices = index.search(query_vector, k=5)

print(f"Nearest neighbors: {indices}")
```

Key Optimization Tips:

- Adjust `nprobe` to balance search speed and accuracy.
- Use precomputed indexes for read-heavy systems to avoid on-the-fly calculations.

Shard and Distribute the Index

For large datasets, split the index across multiple servers (sharding) and use distributed search.

- **Horizontal Scaling:** Distribute retrieval tasks among nodes.
- **Load Balancers:** Use tools like **NGINX** to route queries effectively.

---

2. Leveraging Caching

Cache the results of frequently accessed queries to bypass retrieval entirely for common cases.

Example: Simple Query Cache in Python

python

```
from cachetools import LRUCache

# Initialize a cache with a maximum of 100 items
cache = LRUCache(maxsize=100)
```

```python
def get_retrieval_results(query):
    if query in cache:
        return cache[query]  # Return cached result


    # Simulate a retrieval process
    result = f"Result for '{query}'"
    cache[query] = result  # Cache the new result
    return result
```

```
print(get_retrieval_results("Wha
t is RAG?"))   # Computes and
caches

print(get_retrieval_results("Wha
t is RAG?"))   # Fetches from
cache
```

Benefits:

- Reduces repeated database or retrieval engine calls.
- Improves overall system responsiveness.

Strategies for Reducing Generation Latency

1. Optimize Model Inference

Model Quantization

Reduce the computational overhead by converting model weights to a lower precision (e.g., FP16 or INT8).

Example: Using Quantization with Hugging Face

python

```
from transformers import AutoModelForSeq2SeqLM, AutoTokenizer

from optimum.intel import IncQuantizedModelForSeq2SeqLM
```

```python
# Load a pre-trained model
model_name = "facebook/bart-large"
tokenizer = AutoTokenizer.from_pretrained(model_name)


# Quantize the model
quantized_model = IncQuantizedModelForSeq2SeqLM.from_pretrained(model_name, export=True)


# Generate response with the quantized model
inputs = tokenizer("Explain RAG.", return_tensors="pt")
```

```python
outputs = quantized_model.generate(**inputs)
response = tokenizer.decode(outputs[0], skip_special_tokens=True)

print(response)
```

Batch Inference

Group multiple queries into a batch to reduce overhead and maximize GPU/CPU utilization.

Example: Batched Generation

python

```python
queries = ["What is RAG?",
"Explain dense embeddings.",
"What is FAISS?"]

# Tokenize inputs
tokenized_inputs = tokenizer(queries, return_tensors="pt", padding=True, truncation=True)

# Generate responses in a single batch
batch_outputs = model.generate(**tokenized_inputs)

responses = [tokenizer.decode(output, skip_special_tokens=True) for output in batch_outputs]
```

```
print(responses)
```

2. Leverage Model Distillation

Fine-tune a smaller model to mimic the behavior of a larger, more complex model. This reduces latency while maintaining reasonable accuracy.

Reducing Latency Across the Entire System

1. Asynchronous Processing

Handle retrieval and generation tasks asynchronously to minimize overall processing time.

Example: Async API for Retrieval and Generation

```python
import asyncio

async def retrieve_data(query):
    await asyncio.sleep(0.5)  # Simulate retrieval delay
    return f"Documents for '{query}'"

async def generate_response(retrieved_data):
    await asyncio.sleep(1)  # Simulate generation delay
    return f"Response based on {retrieved_data}"
```

```python
async def process_query(query):
    retrieved_data = await retrieve_data(query)
    response = await generate_response(retrieved_data)
    return response


# Run the async pipeline
query = "What is RAG?"
response = asyncio.run(process_query(query))
print(response)
```

2. Distributed Architectures

Break the system into microservices to distribute the workload effectively. For example:

- Use one service for retrieval and another for generation.
- Deploy both services on auto-scaling infrastructure like AWS ECS or Kubernetes.

---

3. Hardware Acceleration

Use GPUs or TPUs for both retrieval and generation tasks. Inference frameworks like TensorRT can further speed up model execution.

Practical Exercise: Real-Time Latency Reduction

Objective:

Build a chatbot that can respond to user queries in under 500ms.

Steps:

1. **Dataset Preparation:** Prepare a dataset of FAQs and fine-tune a retrieval model.
2. **Infrastructure:**
   - Deploy FAISS for fast retrieval.
   - Use a quantized language model for generation.
3. **Caching:** Implement a caching mechanism for frequently asked questions.
4. **Testing:** Simulate real-time queries using tools like **Locust** or **JMeter**. Measure response times and optimize components.

Summary

This chapter provided actionable strategies for enhancing retrieval accuracy, fine-tuning generative models, scaling RAG systems, and reducing latency. By applying these techniques, you can optimize your RAG implementations for a wide range of advanced applications, from enterprise solutions to real-time systems.

Chapter 7. Best Practices for RAG Development

In this chapter, we delve into key best practices for developing and maintaining Retrieval-Augmented Generation (RAG) systems. These practices address challenges like preventing hallucinations, handling noisy data, ensuring data security, and effectively evaluating and debugging RAG pipelines. By implementing these strategies, you'll enhance the reliability, accuracy, and scalability of your RAG systems.

7.1 Preventing Hallucinations in LLM Outputs

Large Language Models (LLMs) are powerful tools for generating human-like text, but they sometimes produce outputs that are incorrect or fabricated, even when such outputs sound plausible. This issue, often referred to as hallucination, can undermine the reliability of Retrieval-Augmented Generation (RAG) systems. Addressing this challenge involves strategies that align model responses more closely with factual and retrieved evidence.

In this section, we'll explore techniques to minimize hallucinations, supported by clear explanations, practical examples, and well-commented code snippets.

Understanding the Cause of Hallucinations

Hallucinations often occur due to:

1. **Incomplete or irrelevant retrieval results:** The model generates responses without sufficient grounding in the input context.

2. **Over-reliance on training data:** The model draws on its pre-trained knowledge base instead of using provided evidence.
3. **Ambiguous or poorly framed prompts:** If the instructions are unclear, the model might default to plausible-sounding but inaccurate outputs.

By tackling these root causes, we can significantly reduce hallucinations.

Techniques for Preventing Hallucinations

1. Context-Grounded Generation

To ensure accurate outputs, the generation process must be explicitly grounded in the retrieved documents. Use prompts that clearly distinguish between evidence-based responses and speculative ones.

Example: Prompting LLMs with Explicit Context

python

```
from transformers import AutoModelForSeq2SeqLM, AutoTokenizer

# Load a pre-trained model
model_name = "google/flan-t5-large"
tokenizer = AutoTokenizer.from_pretrained(model_name)
model = AutoModelForSeq2SeqLM.from_pretrained(model_name)
```

```python
# Retrieved context
retrieved_context = """
The Eiffel Tower, located in Paris, France, is one of the most iconic structures in the world.
It was completed in 1889 and stands 324 meters tall.
"""


# Query
query = "How tall is the Eiffel Tower?"


# Constructing the input for the model
```

```
input_text = f"Context: {retrieved_context} Query: {query}"

inputs = tokenizer(input_text, return_tensors="pt")


# Generate the response
outputs = model.generate(**inputs, max_length=50)

response = tokenizer.decode(outputs[0], skip_special_tokens=True)


print(response)
```

Explanation:
In this example, the model's output is

anchored to the retrieved context (`retrieved_context`). This ensures the generated response is accurate and grounded in factual evidence.

2. Penalizing Unsupported Claims

Incorporate additional scoring mechanisms to penalize outputs that lack evidence. This can be achieved using confidence scoring models that align outputs with the retrieved content.

3. Fine-Tuning for Domain-Specific Tasks

For domain-specific applications, fine-tune the model on task-relevant datasets. During fine-tuning, provide examples that explicitly penalize unsupported or fabricated responses.

Example: Fine-Tuning a Model

python

```python
from datasets import load_dataset
from transformers import AutoModelForSeq2SeqLM, AutoTokenizer, Seq2SeqTrainer, TrainingArguments

# Load the dataset
dataset = load_dataset("my_domain_specific_dataset")

# Pre-trained model and tokenizer
model_name = "google/flan-t5-base"
```

```python
tokenizer = AutoTokenizer.from_pretrained(model_name)

model = AutoModelForSeq2SeqLM.from_pretrained(model_name)


# Training arguments

training_args = TrainingArguments(

output_dir="./fine_tuned_model",

    evaluation_strategy="epoch",

    save_strategy="epoch",

    learning_rate=2e-5,

per_device_train_batch_size=16,
```

```
    num_train_epochs=3,
    weight_decay=0.01,
)


# Trainer setup
trainer = Seq2SeqTrainer(
    model=model,
    args=training_args,
    train_dataset=dataset["train"],
    eval_dataset=dataset["validation"],
    tokenizer=tokenizer,
)
```

```
# Fine-tuning the model
trainer.train()
```

Explanation:
Fine-tuning helps adapt the model to the specific requirements of a domain, improving the factuality of outputs in specialized tasks.

---

4. Regular Evaluation and Feedback Loops

Continuous evaluation is essential to catch and address hallucinations in production. Use metrics like factual consistency scores to measure performance.

Practical Exercise: Evaluating Outputs

1. Retrieve a set of documents for a predefined query.

2. Generate responses using your RAG pipeline.
3. Manually verify the factual accuracy of the outputs.
4. Log mismatches and refine your system accordingly.

Best Practices for Prompt Design

The quality of the prompt heavily influences the accuracy of the output. A well-designed prompt:

- Specifies the importance of grounding in retrieved content.
- Avoids open-ended speculative queries.
- Provides clear instructions for the desired output format.

Example: Poor vs. Good Prompting

Poor Prompt	Good Prompt
"Tell me about the Eiffel Tower."	"Based on the provided context, what can you tell me about the Eiffel Tower?"

Combining Retrieval and Validation

To enhance reliability, integrate a validation step that compares the generated response against the retrieved evidence. If a mismatch is detected, flag the output for further review.

Example: Basic Validation Workflow

python

```
def validate_output(retrieved_docs, generated_response):
    """
    Validates if the generated response is supported by retrieved documents.
    """
    for doc in retrieved_docs:
        if generated_response.lower() in doc.lower():
            return True
    return False
```

```python
# Example data
retrieved_docs = ["The Eiffel Tower is 324 meters tall.", "It was completed in 1889."]
generated_response = "The Eiffel Tower is 324 meters tall."


# Validate
is_valid = validate_output(retrieved_docs, generated_response)
if is_valid:
    print("The response is valid.")
else:
```

```
    print("The    response    lacks
evidence.")
```

Practical Exercise: Implementing Anti-Hallucination Measures

Objective:

Develop a RAG pipeline that retrieves data and validates outputs for accuracy.

Steps:

1. Set up a simple RAG pipeline with a retrieval and generation component.
2. Implement grounding strategies for context-aware generation.
3. Add a validation step that checks the alignment of outputs with retrieved data.
4. Test with queries that have ambiguous or limited information.

7.2 Handling Noisy and Ambiguous Data

In our world, data is rarely pristine. Whether it's missing values, inconsistent formats, ambiguous language, or outright incorrect entries, noisy and ambiguous data poses a significant challenge for Retrieval-Augmented Generation (RAG) systems. Successfully navigating these challenges is critical for building robust and reliable pipelines.

This chapter delves into practical strategies to handle noisy and ambiguous data effectively. We'll progress from fundamental concepts to advanced techniques, illustrated with examples and code snippets that cater to both beginners and experienced practitioners.

Understanding Noisy and Ambiguous Data

- **Noisy Data:** Data that contains irrelevant, corrupted, or erroneous information.
    - **Examples:** Typographical errors, incorrect labels, incomplete sentences.
- **Ambiguous Data:** Data that is unclear or has multiple interpretations.
    - **Examples:** Vague phrases, conflicting information, or polysemous words (words with multiple meanings).

Strategies for Handling Noisy Data

1. Data Cleaning

Data cleaning involves preprocessing the dataset to remove or correct inconsistencies. Common techniques include:

- **Deduplication:** Remove duplicate records.
- **Normalization:** Standardize formats (e.g., dates, currencies).
- **Error Correction:** Fix spelling errors or incorrect entries.

Example: Cleaning a Dataset

python

```
import pandas as pd

# Example dataset
data = {
    "Name": ["John", "Jhn", "Mary", "Anna", None],
```

```
    "Age": [25, 25, "Twenty-seven", 22, 28],

    "Salary": ["$50,000", "$50,000", "$45k", "50000", None]

}


df = pd.DataFrame(data)

print("Original Data:\n", df)


# Clean the data

df['Name'] = df['Name'].str.title().fillna("Unknown")  # Normalize names

df['Age'] = pd.to_numeric(df['Age'], errors='coerce')  # Convert age to numeric
```

```
df['Salary']                    =
df['Salary'].replace('[\$,k]',
'', regex=True).astype(float)   #
Normalize salary


print("\nCleaned Data:\n", df)
```

Output:

plaintext

```
Original Data:

     Name                      Age
Salary

0    John                       25
$50,000

1    Jhn                        25
$50,000
```

```
2      Mary      Twenty-seven      $45k
3      Anna                        22   50000
4      None                        28   None
```

Cleaned Data:

```
       Name     Age     Salary
0      John     25.0    50000.0
1      Jhn      25.0    50000.0
2      Mary     NaN     45000.0
3      Anna     22.0    50000.0
4      Unknown  28.0    NaN
```

2. Imputation for Missing Data

Missing data can be imputed (filled) with:

- **Mean/Median:** For numeric data.
- **Mode:** For categorical data.
- **Domain-Specific Defaults:** Using values relevant to the context.

Example: Imputing Missing Data

python

```python
# Impute missing values
df['Age'] = df['Age'].fillna(df['Age'].mean())  # Replace NaN with mean age

df['Salary'] = df['Salary'].fillna(40000)  # Replace NaN with default salary
```

```
print("\nData                after
Imputation:\n", df)
```

Strategies for Handling Ambiguous Data

1. Context-Aware Disambiguation

For ambiguous terms, provide additional context to the model to clarify meanings.

Example: Resolving Ambiguity in NLP

python

```
from transformers import pipeline

# Load a question-answering model
```

```python
qa_pipeline = pipeline("question-answering", model="distilbert-base-cased-distilled-squad")


# Ambiguous question
question = "What does Python refer to?"
context = """
Python is both a programming language widely used in software development and a species of large,
nonvenomous snakes found in tropical regions.
"""
```

```
response                       =
qa_pipeline(question=question,
context=context)

print("Resolved    Ambiguity:",
response['answer'])
```

Explanation:
By including both possible meanings in the context, the system can resolve the ambiguity based on the query.

2. Leveraging Domain-Specific Knowledge

Ambiguities can often be resolved by fine-tuning models with domain-specific datasets.

3. Confidence Scoring for Ambiguous Outputs

Assign confidence scores to outputs and flag responses below a threshold for review.

Example: Adding Confidence Scoring

python

```
import numpy as np

# Mock function to simulate scoring
def generate_response_with_score(query, context):
    response = "Python refers to a programming language."
```

```python
    score = np.random.uniform(0.7, 0.9)  # Simulated confidence score
    return response, score


query = "What is Python?"
context = "Python can refer to programming or a snake."

response, score = generate_response_with_score(query, context)
if score < 0.8:
    print("Low confidence: Review response manually.")
else:
    print("Response:", response)
```

```
    print("Confidence    Score:", 
score)
```

Integrating Noise and Ambiguity Handling in RAG Pipelines

RAG pipelines must accommodate noisy and ambiguous data during retrieval and generation.

Pipeline Components:

1. **Preprocessing Module:** Cleans and formats input data.
2. **Retrieval Engine:** Filters out irrelevant or low-quality documents.
3. **Generation Component:** Generates outputs with grounding in retrieved data.
4. **Validation Layer:** Ensures outputs align with retrieved evidence.

Example: Simple RAG Pipeline

python

```
def preprocess_query(query):
    """Cleans and normalizes the input query."""
    return query.lower().strip()


def retrieve_documents(query, corpus):
    """Retrieves relevant documents based on a query."""
    return [doc for doc in corpus if query in doc.lower()]


def generate_response(query, documents):
```

```
    """Generates a response grounded in retrieved documents."""
    context = " ".join(documents)
    return f"Based on the context: {context}, the answer is ..."


# Example usage
query = "python programming"
corpus = [
    "Python is a programming language.",
    "Python is a type of snake found in the wild."
]
```

```
query = preprocess_query(query)

retrieved_docs = retrieve_documents(query, corpus)

response = generate_response(query, retrieved_docs)


print("Query:", query)

print("Retrieved Documents:", retrieved_docs)

print("Response:", response)
```

Practical Exercise: Building a Resilient Data Pipeline

Objective:

Develop a pipeline that:

1. Handles noisy inputs.
2. Resolves ambiguities using context.
3. Validates outputs for consistency.

Steps:

1. Create a noisy dataset with ambiguous entries.
2. Implement preprocessing to clean the dataset.
3. Design a retrieval engine with confidence scoring.
4. Test the pipeline with edge cases to ensure reliability.

7.3 Securing Sensitive Data in RAG Pipelines

Data security is paramount in Retrieval-Augmented Generation (RAG) pipelines, especially when dealing with sensitive or confidential information. Whether it's personal health records, financial data, or proprietary business documents, ensuring the privacy and security of this data is essential. This chapter will guide you through best practices for securing sensitive data in RAG pipelines, with practical examples and hands-on exercises.

Understanding the Risks

Before implementing security measures, it's essential to understand the risks associated with RAG pipelines:

1. **Unauthorized Access:** Sensitive data can be exposed if access controls are not stringent.
2. **Data Leakage:** Unintended sharing of confidential information in outputs.
3. **Model Exploitation:** Attackers extracting sensitive information by querying models repeatedly.
4. **Compliance Violations:** Failure to meet regulations such as GDPR, HIPAA, or CCPA.

---

1. Implementing Access Controls

Access controls ensure that only authorized users or systems can access sensitive data.

Best Practices

- Use **Role-Based Access Control (RBAC)** to restrict access.

- Encrypt data at rest and in transit using strong encryption standards like AES-256 or TLS 1.2+.

Example: Configuring Access Control in a Database

python

```
import sqlite3

# Connect to a secure database
conn = sqlite3.connect('secure_data.db')

# Create a table with restricted access
conn.execute('''
```

```
CREATE TABLE IF NOT EXISTS sensitive_data (

    id INTEGER PRIMARY KEY,

    name TEXT NOT NULL,

    sensitive_info TEXT NOT NULL

);
''')


# Example of inserting encrypted data

from cryptography.fernet import Fernet


# Generate a key and encrypt sensitive info

key = Fernet.generate_key()
```

```python
cipher = Fernet(key)
encrypted_data = cipher.encrypt(b"This is sensitive information.")


# Insert encrypted data
conn.execute('INSERT INTO sensitive_data (name, sensitive_info) VALUES (?, ?)',
             ('John Doe', encrypted_data.decode()))
conn.commit()


# Access control: Only authorized users should have access to the key
print("Encryption Key (Store securely):", key.decode())
```

```
conn.close()
```

2. Preventing Data Leakage

Models should not inadvertently reveal sensitive data in their outputs.

Techniques

- **Fine-Tune with Sanitized Data:** Ensure training data does not include sensitive details.
- **Output Filtering:** Implement post-processing steps to remove sensitive information from responses.
- **Differential Privacy:** Introduce controlled noise to outputs to prevent exact reconstruction of sensitive data.

Example: Filtering Model Outputs

python

```
from transformers import pipeline

# Load a pre-trained pipeline
generator = pipeline("text-generation", model="gpt-2")

# Define sensitive terms to redact
sensitive_terms = ["John Doe", "123-45-6789"]

# Generate a response and filter sensitive terms
```

```python
response = generator("My social security number is 123-45-6789.", max_length=30)
filtered_response = response[0]['generated_text']


# Redact sensitive terms
for term in sensitive_terms:
    filtered_response = filtered_response.replace(term, "[REDACTED]")


print("Filtered Response:", filtered_response)
```

3. Securing Data in Transit

Data transmitted between components of a RAG pipeline must be protected from interception.

Techniques

- Use **TLS (Transport Layer Security)** for all API communications.
- Implement **authentication mechanisms** like OAuth2 for APIs.

Example: Secure API Communication

python

```
import requests

# Example of making a secure API call
url = "https://secure-api.example.com/data"
```

```python
headers = {
    "Authorization": "Bearer YOUR_ACCESS_TOKEN",
    "Content-Type": "application/json"
}


response = requests.get(url, headers=headers)
if response.status_code == 200:
    print("Secure Data Retrieved:", response.json())
else:
    print("Failed to retrieve data securely.")
```

4. Protecting Against Model Exploitation

Attackers might exploit RAG models to infer sensitive details by submitting multiple queries. Techniques like **adversarial queries** or **membership inference attacks** are common.

Defenses

- **Rate Limiting:** Restrict the number of queries per user.
- **Monitoring and Logging:** Detect unusual activity patterns.
- **Model Watermarking:** Identify and prevent unauthorized usage.

Example: Implementing Rate Limiting

python

```python
from flask import Flask, request, jsonify
from time import time


app = Flask(__name__)
user_requests = {}


@app.route('/query', methods=['POST'])
def query_model():
    user_id = request.headers.get("User-ID")
    current_time = time()

    # Initialize user request log
```

```
    if user_id not in user_requests:
        user_requests[user_id] = []

    # Filter out old requests
    user_requests[user_id] = [t for t in user_requests[user_id] if current_time - t < 60]

    # Enforce rate limit
    if len(user_requests[user_id]) >= 5:
        return jsonify({"error": "Rate limit exceeded. Try again later."}), 429
```

```python
    # Log current request
    user_requests[user_id].append(current_time)

    # Process the query
    return jsonify({"response": "Model response goes here."})

if __name__ == '__main__':
    app.run()
```

---

5. Ensuring Regulatory Compliance

Compliance with data protection laws is critical for RAG systems handling sensitive data.

Steps to Achieve Compliance

- **Data Minimization:** Only collect data strictly necessary for processing.
- **Audit Trails:** Maintain logs to demonstrate adherence to regulations.
- **User Consent:** Obtain explicit consent for data usage when required.

Example: Logging Data Access

python

```
import logging

# Configure logging
logging.basicConfig(filename="access_log.txt",
level=logging.INFO)
```

```
def log_access(user_id, action):
    logging.info(f"User: {user_id}, Action: {action}, Timestamp: {time()}")


# Simulate logging a data access event
log_access("user123", "Accessed sensitive data.")
```

Practical Exercise: Building a Secure RAG Pipeline

Objective

Design a secure RAG pipeline that:

1. Encrypts sensitive data during storage and transmission.
2. Filters outputs to prevent leakage.
3. Implements rate limiting to protect against exploitation.

Steps

1. Set up a database with encrypted storage for sensitive documents.
2. Build an API layer with authentication and TLS.
3. Integrate a model with output filtering and logging.
4. Test with adversarial queries and monitor logs for anomalies.

7.4 Evaluating and Debugging RAG Systems

Building robust Retrieval-Augmented Generation (RAG) systems is a complex task. While performance optimization and deployment are critical steps, evaluating and debugging the system effectively ensures its accuracy, reliability, and scalability. This chapter walks you through the essentials of evaluating and debugging RAG systems, using systematic approaches, practical tools, and real-world examples.

Key Metrics for Evaluating RAG Systems

Before diving into debugging, we need to establish clear evaluation metrics. These help assess how well the RAG system is performing across retrieval and generation components.

1. **Retrieval Metrics**
    - **Precision@k**: Measures the proportion of relevant documents in the top-k retrieved results.

- **Recall@k**: Evaluates how many of the relevant documents are included in the top-k results.

2. **Generation Metrics**
    - **BLEU (Bilingual Evaluation Understudy)**: Quantifies the overlap between generated and reference text.
    - **ROUGE (Recall-Oriented Understudy for Gisting Evaluation)**: Measures recall-based overlap, useful for summarization.
    - **Perplexity**: Indicates how well the language model predicts the next word. Lower perplexity signifies better performance.

3. **End-to-End Metrics**
    - **Response Time**: Total time taken for the system to return a response.

- **Accuracy**: Percentage of user queries successfully answered.
- **User Feedback**: Metrics from surveys or interaction logs to assess usability and relevance.

Step 1: Evaluating the Retrieval Component

The retrieval system is the foundation of RAG pipelines. If it retrieves irrelevant documents, the generated output will suffer.

Example: Evaluating with Precision and Recall

python

```python
from sklearn.metrics import precision_score, recall_score

# Sample ground truth and predicted labels
true_relevant = [1, 0, 1, 1, 0]
predicted_relevant = [1, 0, 1, 0, 0]

# Calculate precision and recall
precision = precision_score(true_relevant, predicted_relevant)
recall = recall_score(true_relevant, predicted_relevant)
```

```
print(f"Precision: {precision:.2f}")

print(f"Recall: {recall:.2f}")
```

Practical Tip

If precision is high but recall is low, the system may be overly conservative, retrieving fewer documents. Conversely, high recall but low precision means it retrieves too many irrelevant documents. Strike a balance by tuning retrieval thresholds.

Step 2: Evaluating the Generation Component

Assessing the language model's outputs involves automated and human-in-the-loop evaluation.

Automated Evaluation with ROUGE

python

```
from rouge_score import rouge_scorer

# Reference and generated text
reference = "The capital of France is Paris."
generated = "Paris is the capital of France."

# Calculate ROUGE scores
```

```
scorer = rouge_scorer.RougeScorer(['rouge1', 'rougeL'], use_stemmer=True)

scores = scorer.score(reference, generated)

print("ROUGE-1:", scores['rouge1'])
print("ROUGE-L:", scores['rougeL'])
```

Human Evaluation

Ask evaluators to rate outputs based on:

1. **Relevance:** Does the answer align with the query?
2. **Fluency:** Is the response grammatically correct and coherent?

3. **Factuality:** Is the response accurate?

Step 3: Debugging Retrieval Failures

Common Issues

1. **Low Recall:** Important documents are missing from the top-k results.
2. **High Irrelevance:** The retrieved documents are unrelated to the query.

Solution: Query Reformulation

Query reformulation involves rewriting user queries for better matching with indexed documents. Tools like BM25 and dense retrievers can assist.

python

```
from rank_bm25 import BM25Okapi
```

```python
# Sample corpus and query
corpus = ["The Eiffel Tower is in Paris.",
          "Berlin is the capital of Germany.",
          "London is a city in the UK."]
query = "capital of Germany"


# Tokenize corpus and query
tokenized_corpus = [doc.split(" ") for doc in corpus]
bm25 = BM25Okapi(tokenized_corpus)
```

```
scores = bm25.get_scores(query.split(" "))

# Retrieve the best match
best_match_index = scores.argmax()
print("Best Match:", corpus[best_match_index])
```

Step 4: Debugging Generation Failures

Issue 1: Hallucinations

Hallucinations occur when the model generates information not present in the retrieved documents.

Fix:

- Use stricter conditioning on retrieved documents by appending them to the input prompt.
- Experiment with smaller decoding temperatures during text generation.

Example: Adjusting Decoding Temperature

python

```
from transformers import GPT2LMHeadModel, GPT2Tokenizer

# Load the model and tokenizer
model_name = "gpt2"
```

```python
tokenizer = GPT2Tokenizer.from_pretrained(model_name)
model = GPT2LMHeadModel.from_pretrained(model_name)


# Input prompt
prompt = "The capital of Germany is"
input_ids = tokenizer(prompt, return_tensors="pt").input_ids


# Generate with different temperatures
outputs = model.generate(input_ids, max_length=20, temperature=0.5)
```

```python
print(tokenizer.decode(outputs[0], skip_special_tokens=True))
```

Step 5: Logging and Monitoring

Integrate robust logging systems to trace errors and understand system behavior.

Example: Logging API Requests

python

```python
import logging

# Configure logging
logging.basicConfig(filename="rag_logs.txt", level=logging.INFO)
```

```
def log_request(query, response, status):
    logging.info(f"Query: {query}, Response: {response}, Status: {status}")


# Simulate a query-response log
log_request("What is the capital of France?", "The capital of France is Paris.", "Success")
```

Step 6: Continuous Evaluation

RAG systems evolve as new data and use cases emerge. Regular evaluation ensures that performance remains consistent over time.

A/B Testing

Deploy multiple versions of your pipeline (e.g., with different retrievers or models) to compare performance metrics and user satisfaction.

Practical Exercise: Debugging a Sample RAG System

Objective

Debug a RAG system suffering from low recall and hallucinations.

1. Evaluate retrieval accuracy using precision and recall metrics.
2. Implement query reformulation to improve document retrieval.
3. Adjust generation settings to reduce hallucinations.

Steps

1. Create a dataset with known queries and expected answers.
2. Run evaluations on the current system.
3. Apply the fixes outlined in this chapter and re-evaluate.
4. Document the improvements.

Conclusion

Mastering best practices for RAG development ensures your system is robust, secure, and user-focused. By addressing hallucinations, handling noisy data, securing sensitive pipelines, and implementing thorough evaluation and debugging processes, you can build RAG systems that are both reliable and efficient.

Chapter 8. Future Directions for RAG

The field of Retrieval-Augmented Generation (RAG) is rapidly evolving, fueled by advances in AI research, practical applications, and a growing understanding of the ethical implications surrounding its use. This chapter explores the emerging trends shaping RAG, including integrating multimodal data, breakthroughs in embedding models and search algorithms, and the importance of addressing ethical considerations such as bias, privacy, and responsible AI practices.

8.1 Emerging Trends in Retrieval-Augmented Generation

RAG systems are expanding beyond conventional text retrieval and generation tasks. Emerging trends point toward more robust, efficient, and context-aware applications.

1. Context-Aware Retrieval

Next-generation RAG systems aim to enhance context awareness, enabling them to retrieve and generate information based on nuanced user intent.

Example: Personalizing a virtual assistant's responses based on a user's interaction history.

python

```
# Example: Contextual Retrieval with User-Specific Data
user_query = "What's the weather?"
user_location = "New York"
```

```python
# Simulating retrieval based on user-specific context
def retrieve_weather_data(query, location):
    if location == "New York":
        return "It's sunny in New York with a high of 75°F."
    return "Location not found."

response = retrieve_weather_data(user_query, user_location)
print(response)
```

2. Real-Time Collaboration

RAG systems are now being used in collaborative tools, allowing multiple users to interact with the same system for group decision-making, document drafting, or brainstorming sessions.

3. Domain-Specific Applications

Tailored RAG models are being developed for industries like healthcare, law, and education. These systems rely on specialized datasets and fine-tuning to improve accuracy and relevance.

8.2 Integrating Multimodal Data with RAG

Multimodal RAG systems combine text, images, and videos to retrieve and generate richer, more comprehensive outputs. These systems are crucial for applications in media, e-commerce, and education.

Challenges

- **Representation**: Encoding diverse data types in a unified format.
- **Fusion**: Combining insights from text, images, and videos into a coherent output.

Example: Multimodal Retrieval in E-Commerce

A user searches for "comfortable running shoes" while uploading an image of their current pair. The system retrieves recommendations based on textual preferences and visual similarity.

python

```
from transformers import CLIPProcessor, CLIPModel
```

```python
# Load a multimodal model like CLIP
model = CLIPModel.from_pretrained("openai/clip-vit-base-patch32")
processor = CLIPProcessor.from_pretrained("openai/clip-vit-base-patch32")


# Example text and image inputs
text = ["comfortable running shoes"]
image_path = "current_shoes.jpg"


# Preprocess inputs
inputs = processor(text=text, images=image_path,
```

```
                return_tensors="pt",
                padding=True)

# Get embeddings
outputs = model(**inputs)
print("Text and image embeddings generated successfully!")
```

Applications of Multimodal RAG

1. **Content Creation**: Generating product descriptions with accompanying visuals.
2. **Healthcare**: Interpreting medical images with textual explanations.
3. **Education**: Creating interactive learning materials using videos, text, and images.

8.3 Advances in Embedding Models and Search Algorithms

Embedding models and search algorithms are the backbone of RAG systems. Recent advancements focus on improving accuracy, efficiency, and scalability.

1. Dense Embeddings with Knowledge Distillation

Modern dense embeddings are optimized for specific domains using knowledge distillation techniques, which reduce computational complexity without compromising performance.

Example: Fine-Tuning Dense Embeddings

python

```python
from sentence_transformers import SentenceTransformer, InputExample, losses
from torch.utils.data import DataLoader

# Load a pre-trained model
model = SentenceTransformer('sentence-transformers/all-MiniLM-L6-v2')

# Prepare fine-tuning data
train_examples = [InputExample(texts=["Document 1", "Relevant snippet"], label=1),

InputExample(texts=["Document
```

```
2", "Irrelevant snippet"], label=0)]


train_dataloader = DataLoader(train_examples, shuffle=True, batch_size=16)

train_loss = losses.CosineSimilarityLoss(model)


# Fine-tune model

model.fit(train_objectives=[(train_dataloader, train_loss)], epochs=1, warmup_steps=100)

print("Fine-tuning complete!")
```

2. Approximate Nearest Neighbor (ANN) Search

ANN algorithms like FAISS significantly speed up large-scale retrieval tasks by approximating nearest neighbors.

8.4 Ethical Considerations: Bias, Privacy, and Responsible AI

As RAG systems become more pervasive, addressing ethical issues is critical to ensure fairness, accountability, and transparency.

1. Mitigating Bias

RAG systems inherit biases from training data, potentially amplifying stereotypes or excluding minority perspectives. To counteract this:

- Use diverse and representative datasets.

- Implement fairness-aware algorithms.

Example: Detecting Bias in Outputs

python

```
def detect_bias(output):
    biased_keywords = ["gender-specific", "racial"]
    for word in biased_keywords:
        if word in output.lower():
            return "Potential bias detected!"
    return "Output is bias-free."

# Test case
```

```
response = "Only men can perform this task."
print(detect_bias(response))
```

2. Ensuring Privacy

Protecting sensitive user data is non-negotiable, especially in healthcare, finance, and legal applications. Techniques like differential privacy and secure multi-party computation help achieve this.

3. Promoting Transparency

Explainable AI (XAI) principles enable users to understand how RAG systems make decisions.

4. Responsible AI Development

Adopting guidelines from frameworks like the AI Ethics Guidelines by OECD or principles from the EU's AI Act ensures compliance and builds user trust.

Conclusion

The future of Retrieval-Augmented Generation is promising, with advancements in multimodal integration, embedding technologies, and ethical AI practices paving the way for innovative applications. By staying informed about these trends and applying the techniques shared in this chapter, developers can build cutting-edge RAG systems that are not only powerful but also responsible and inclusive.

Chapter 9. Appendix

This appendix serves as a practical resource for developers, researchers, and enthusiasts of Retrieval-Augmented Generation (RAG). It includes downloadable code snippets, templates for common workflows, recommended resources, and a glossary of essential terms. Whether you're revisiting key concepts or diving into advanced implementations, this chapter is designed to complement your journey in building efficient RAG systems.

9.1 Code Snippets and Examples

This section features code snippets and ready-to-use templates to help streamline your RAG development process.

Downloadable Code for RAG Implementation

The following code demonstrates a simplified implementation of a RAG pipeline that retrieves information and generates context-aware responses.

python

```
from transformers import AutoTokenizer, AutoModelForSeq2SeqLM

from sentence_transformers import SentenceTransformer

from sklearn.metrics.pairwise import cosine_similarity


# Load pre-trained models
```

```python
retriever = SentenceTransformer('sentence-transformers/all-MiniLM-L6-v2')

tokenizer = AutoTokenizer.from_pretrained("facebook/bart-large")

generator = AutoModelForSeq2SeqLM.from_pretrained("facebook/bart-large")


# Sample documents

documents = [
    "Python is a versatile programming language.",
    "Transformers are state-of-the-art models in NLP.",
    "RAG combines retrieval and generation effectively."
```

```
]


# Embedding documents

doc_embeddings = retriever.encode(documents)


# User query

query = "What is RAG?"

query_embedding = retriever.encode([query])


# Find the most relevant document

similarities = cosine_similarity([query_embedding], doc_embeddings)
```

```python
most_relevant_idx = similarities.argmax()

retrieved_doc = documents[most_relevant_idx]


# Generate response using the retrieved document

input_text = f"Document: {retrieved_doc} Query: {query}"

input_ids = tokenizer(input_text, return_tensors="pt", truncation=True, padding=True).input_ids

output = generator.generate(input_ids)
```

```
response = tokenizer.decode(output[0], skip_special_tokens=True)


print("Query:", query)

print("Retrieved Document:", retrieved_doc)

print("Generated Response:", response)
```

Ready-to-Use Templates for Common RAG Workflows

1. **Template for Domain-Specific RAG Fine-Tuning**

Fine-tune RAG systems for a specific domain using custom datasets.

python

```
from transformers import RagTokenizer, RagRetriever, RagSequenceForGeneration

# Load RAG model components
tokenizer = RagTokenizer.from_pretrained("facebook/rag-token-nq")
retriever = RagRetriever.from_pretrained("facebook/rag-token-nq")
```

```python
model = RagSequenceForGeneration.from_pretrained("facebook/rag-token-nq", retriever=retriever)


# Custom training data
context = "Healthcare-related documents"
query = "What are the symptoms of diabetes?"


# Tokenization
input_dict = tokenizer.prepare_seq2seq_batch(query=query, context=context, return_tensors="pt")
```

```
# Train or fine-tune the model

output = model(**input_dict)

print("Fine-tuning complete!")
```

2. **Template for Multimodal RAG Integration**

Extend RAG functionality to work with multimodal data (text and images).

python

```
from transformers import CLIPProcessor, CLIPModel

# Load CLIP model
```

```python
model = CLIPModel.from_pretrained("openai/clip-vit-base-patch32")
processor = CLIPProcessor.from_pretrained("openai/clip-vit-base-patch32")


# Inputs
text_inputs = ["A picture of a dog."]
image_path = "dog.jpg"


# Process inputs
inputs = processor(text=text_inputs, images=image_path, return_tensors="pt", padding=True)
```

```
outputs = model(**inputs)

print("Generated embeddings for text and image!")
```

9.2 Resources and References

Popular Tools and Libraries for Practitioners

1. **Transformers by Hugging Face**: A versatile library for pre-trained models in NLP.
2. **FAISS by Facebook AI**: A library for efficient similarity search and clustering.
3. **LangChain**: A framework for building RAG pipelines with ease.

4. **Sentence-Transformers**: Models for dense embeddings and semantic search.
5. **ONNX Runtime**: Optimize RAG models for production.

9.3 Glossary of Terms

Key Terminology for RAG and NLP

1. **Retrieval-Augmented Generation (RAG):** A hybrid NLP approach that retrieves external knowledge to enhance text generation.
2. **Dense Embeddings:** High-dimensional vector representations of text, optimized for semantic similarity.
3. **Sparse Embeddings:** Traditional text vectorization methods like TF-IDF or bag-of-words.
4. **Generative Pre-trained Transformer (GPT):** A model

architecture for generating coherent and context-aware text.
5. **Multimodal Data:** Data involving multiple formats, such as text, images, and videos.
6. **Fine-Tuning:** Adjusting a pre-trained model for a specific domain or task.
7. **Hallucination:** When a model generates outputs that are plausible but factually incorrect.
8. **Latency:** The time delay between a user request and the system's response.
9. **Explainability:** The ability to understand and interpret a model's outputs.
10. **Approximate Nearest Neighbor (ANN):** Algorithms that speed up the search for similar vectors in large datasets.

This appendix provides the tools and knowledge necessary for exploring and implementing RAG systems. From practical code templates to curated resources and a glossary of terms, it serves as a comprehensive guide for both beginners and advanced practitioners. Keep this section bookmarked for quick reference as you continue your journey in the dynamic field of Retrieval-Augmented Generation.